The author, Fotis Loizou, was born in Stylloi, Cyprus. He, along with his parents and sister, immigrated to England in 1957. He is a graduate of London University and has taught English Language and Literature in secondary schools for over 25 years. During his spare time, he paints, gardens, reads and writes stories and poems.

'One Way Ticket: The Autobiography of a London Cypriot' is the longest narrative he has attempted to date. It is also the first work that he has decided to submit for publication.

For my parents, Adriana and Loizos.

Fotis Loizou

ONE WAY TICKET: THE AUTOBIOGRAPHY OF A LONDON CYPRIOT

AUSTIN MACAULEY PUBLISHERS™

LONDON · CAMBRIDGE · NEW YORK · SHARJAH

A CIP catalogue record for this title is available from the British Library.

ISBN 9781528934664 (Paperback)
ISBN 9781528967969 (ePub e-book)

www.austinmacauley.com

First Published (2019)
Austin Macauley Publishers Ltd
25 Canada Square
Canary Wharf
London
E14 5LQ

I would like to thank my dearest wife, Valeriya Loizou, for her assistance that she provided during the course of writing this book.

Part 1: Roots

Mother

My mother awoke
before the birds
had sung
their mornings melodies.
She awoke
in the early morning darkness
with the star
of dawn still
flickering
in the falling
night sky,
while in motionless morning
sweet sleep,
as if from carved, cool,
mellow marble,
we deeply dreamed.

She dressed quickly,
a coarse skirt,
a plain blouse,
a pair of worn shoes.
She bathed her face
in clean, cool,
refreshing water,
combed
her silky, soft, straight,
black hair,
could have been
an actress
or a celebrity
in another place,
in another time.
No need for make up

in her present circumstances,
in her stark reality,
like the morning
sun
that peeped
over
the dark horizon.
No young woman's
fantasies here
for the Parisian
or London look,
once glimpsed
in a fashion magazine,
in a house
that she cleaned,
scrubbed and polished.
Rough hands,
Split fingernails
For a piece of bread,
a cup of water,
her morning sustenance.

At the *baranga** door
she glanced back
at us
before
stepping out
– a silent silhouette
against a morning
orange sky.

~

Four Miles

Mother was working for English service families at 'Four Miles'. She cleaned their houses from morning until night. I was hardly more than an infant and she would leave me at home to be looked after by my sister who was only a child herself. The 1950s was a time of economic hardship in Cyprus and sometimes people went hungry because they didn't have enough money to buy what they needed. When people who are suffering deprivations feel that there is no hope of improving themselves, they will look beyond their shores or their borders to places that might provide a more hopeful future. This has always been the case, both now and in the past. With this in mind, Father had already gone abroad to seek some solution to the economic difficulties we were faced with. He and thousands of other Cypriots, who left the island at that time, were searching for a better life, looking for hope, exploring the possibilities to better themselves. Mother was left behind to work, if there was any work to be had and to bring up my sister and me. Such was life for the ordinary Cypriot in the mid-1950s.

Cyprus was a small cornerstone of the British Empire, the empire upon which the sun never set but was, in fact, now crumbling, crumbling in Africa and crumbling in Asia. Is it to be believed that any colonial power can be a force for good? The Cypriots, like many other people who have endured colonialism might doubt it, for even though the British Lion had annexed Cyprus in 1914, the Cypriot people were still suffering great economic hardships. In fact, the people of Cyprus had not gained anything by the transfer of ownership of the island from the Ottoman turban to the British Crown. Cyprus had been exploited by both colonial powers and most of its people continued to live from hand to mouth. It was only the few who had enough to eat; it was only the few whose children could attend school beyond the primary level and it was only the few who could look forward to life with some kind of optimism. The majority, the hoi polloi[1] were left to struggle with hunger, illiteracy and hardship.

How difficult Mother's life must have been! How she must have suffered! It seems that most mothers, no matter where they are, face the same problem of who is to look after the children to enable them to work.

In every city in the world, you can notice the mothers of young children wheeling prams early in the morning, desperately hurrying, on their way to the baby-minder or to a nursery before rushing to work.

My mother thought that she had discovered the perfect solution to the problem. She enrolled me at a newly opened nursery. She had a lot of pride and wanted to do things independently, not to ask for help from her relatives. So she worked harder, she worked faster, cleaned two or three houses more every day and she worked without pause from morning until night. They paid her a few shillings for her labour, unable to believe how cheap all that mundane work was that they would have to have done themselves in their terraced and semis back in England. She worked very hard so she could pay for the nursery fee, to feed and to clothe us, she worked for her dignity and she worked because it was the only thing she had ever known in her life. She wanted us to be as good as anybody else but she had to earn that privilege with the sweat of her brow.

On one particular day, she tried to do more than she could handle in the given time; she was late for the bus that would have enabled her to collect me on time from the nursery. I remember that day like a dream. All the children had been collected by their parents and I was left alone with the sombre family who were the nursery proprietors. They sat waiting without speaking and even though I was only four or five years old, I sensed that they were in some way very annoyed and so I played silently without daring to look up at their stern faces. Time seemed to move slowly, slowly like an old lady with a walking stick. I couldn't tell the time but I kept looking at the big clock in the adjacent hall, listening to its rhythmic ticking. *Tick, tock, tick, tock.* It went on relentlessly without stopping, ceaselessly without end. The more I listened, the more confused, perplexed, unhappy I became. I was in a panic: would my mother not return? Had she forgotten all about me? Was I going to be left with Mr Nicholas and his wife forever?

"She's late, she's always going to be late! Nico, we can't tolerate this," nagged the wife of the proprietor. "The next thing will be that she won't be able to pay. This nursery is beyond her means and you should get rid of them now."

They conversed loudly and occasionally looked in my direction. I was able to hear their words. I felt their unpleasantness and hostility. Mr Nicholas was not going to argue with his wife. He surrendered to her demands and he was going to deal with the matter without any objections.

At long last, my mother arrived. I could hear her footsteps approaching from the darkness outside. I knew it was her; how could she have left me for so long with these unsmiling people? I was angry, my tears were welling up in my eyes, but when I saw her, I ran to her as if she was my liberator. She was my hero who was going to take me away from the morose Mr Nicholas and his angry little wife. Mother hardly spoke to me. She immediately addressed the proprietor in an apologetic voice.

"I am sorry, Mr Nicholas. I had so much work… and I missed my bus… I am so sorry for making you wait and keeping you all from your rest."

Mr Nicholas had a fat, perspiring face with a small, spiky moustache, a moustache that made him look rather clownish, even though he tried to look like an important man who had been wronged. He spoke in a very quiet, subdued, serious manner, as if he was a doctor with bad news.

"Mrs Loizou, you are not late by only a few minutes, but by more than an hour!"

His voice rose to a higher note on the last syllable as if to add emphasis to what he was saying.

"I can see," he continued, "it is going to be a problem getting here on time to collect your child and this is very difficult for us because we are tired and we have other things to do."

He looked a little embarrassed at having to play the role of a harder person than what he actually was and nervously glanced at his little wife who was sitting tense and silent on one side of the porch, observing the unfolding events but not saying a word. My mother understood that the little woman hiding behind him had been goading him on to be as severe as possible. My mother was not prepared to change her plans just yet and insisted on the agreed arrangement. Despite her tiredness, she found the strength to at least try some negotiation. She was not one to walk away from a challenge.

"Mr Nicholas, I have only been this late just this one time and I promise you it will not happen again. It was unforeseen, the lady who I work for on this day had some very important unexpected guests and she pleaded with me to stay an extra two hours for double the hourly rate… I can give you some extra money for the additional hour that my child has been with you."

She then started to desperately search her handbag for the money that she had received on that day, took out some notes and thrust them at Mr Nicholas who raised his palms as if to defend himself. He spoke quietly but firmly while his little wife now standing behind him looked very annoyed with my mother's audacity. How dare this peasant woman not understand what she was being told! How dare she throw her pennies at them! How dare she raise her voice with such impudence! But still, she remained silent, hidden, diminutive. She didn't say anything.

"No, Mrs Loizou, this is not about money, but it is about being able to pick up your child on time. I also have to think of the other people who work with me because they need to be released from their duties after a long working day. I am sorry… I also sometimes have a tight schedule and I depend on the parents picking up their children on time. You just haven't been able to do that."

By the end of his little speech, his troubled face, full of annoyance, was perspiring profusely and Mother realised that Mr Nicholas was not going to be allowed to change his mind. Behind him, his little wife, with her tight thin lips and round little eyes, felt triumphant.

Without saying another word, Mother took me by the hand and we both walked out of the nursery. Soon after, Mother withdrew from the nursery. She had decided to ask Grandmother to look after me. She wanted me to attend the nursery but as it turned out, on this occasion, mother's plan had not come to fruition.

~

We travelled by bus from Varosi[2] where we lived in a baranga, a type of wooden house, near the sea front. We caught the bus from the bus station in the centre of town. As soon as we boarded the bus, we began to immediately perspire. It felt hot and airless like an oven. Despite this, the bus soon filled with people from the village who had been conducting their business in town and were now in a hurry to return home before the intense heat of the early afternoon. There were three or four students from the Varosi gymnasium, the main secondary school of the town, who were easily recognisable by their peaked, military style, high school caps and who, despite the heat, were engaged in animated discussion. Some village house wives sat at the rear of the bus. They had probably attended to various essential matters in town or perhaps had been shopping for some items that couldn't be found in the village shop. They talked quietly amongst themselves and sometimes modest laughter could be heard coming from them. Some other people sat alone, without speaking with anyone, waiting patiently, sometimes with closed eyes, for the bus journey to begin.

The bus driver, a big, middle-aged man with an extended girth, a bald head and a Zapata moustache eventually took his seat, and with a turn of the ignition key, the old engine of the ancient bus made a great cranking noise; it grumbled and grunted into reluctant motion. The tired, old bus began to make its way slowly through the narrow streets of Varosi, clanking, coughing and spewing black exhaust fumes, heading for Stylloi[3], a village of the Mesaoria Plain, on the road between Famagusta and Nicosia.

On our outward journey, we passed by the broad and bulky Venetian walls[4], walls that had for a time successfully defended the city from the Ottoman siege in the 16th century until the defenders were forced by hunger, thirst and starvation to surrender to the invaders. Behind them live to this day, the Turkish Cypriot citizens of Famagusta's old city who, at that time, only reluctantly ventured beyond their protection. The demand for Enosis, union with Greece, by the Greek Cypriots was rapidly becoming a serious crisis. From hindsight, we know that this policy was a great error that has led to disaster and suffering. When there are naïve and weak leaders, leaders who cannot comprehend events, leaders who are unable to read the signs of what is coming, then the afflictions of chaos, confusion and conflict reign supreme in the land. Such a fate awaited our beloved island.

The old bus slowly accelerated, moving beyond the shadow of the city walls and into the open countryside.

We journeyed from the town to the village on a day of brilliant, bright, cutting sunshine and cloudless blue skies. The burning heat drained our energy; it was intense, oppressive, an assault on our physical endurance making our bodies feel heavy and sleepy. The animated discussion of the gymnasium students gradually lost its momentum and then fizzled out. The housewives in the rear had stopped talking and each one of them was now immersed in her own private thoughts. The passengers, who sat alone, had either fallen asleep or were gazing aimlessly out of the window. With each passing mile, our journey grew in discomfort. We passed through a landscape of sun-scorched grass dotted here and there with wrinkled olive trees. Occasionally, we glimpsed some isolated figures working in the fields. They seemed tiny on a huge landscape, working under a clear blue sky, relentlessly being beaten by a harsh, merciless summer sun.

The scene could have been from a thousand years ago; it was the timeless engagement of men toiling to bring forth fruit from the soil, a soil that had been soaked with the blood and sweat of its people, a soil that had been fought over, contested and claimed by invaders and conquerors but which rarely ever belonged to those who worked upon it.

When our bus drew parallel with the figures on the landscape, they would look up and wave as the old bus trundled along the uneven road, churning clouds of dust in its wake. The journey was short, just a few miles from Varosi, but we felt as if we were being shaken, tossed and turned for an eternity, every time the wheels went over a hole in the road.

Eventually, the bus stopped outside the Stylloi café, in the centre of the tiny village which was no more than a cluster of white-washed houses built around a few narrow streets that seemed particularly isolated during

17

the heat of the day when people took cover indoors or wherever shade might be found from the blistering heat.

We alighted from the bus feeling tired and bedraggled. We were too hot to even speak to each other; we walked in a parched silence along the dusty dirt road that led to my grandmother's house that was just a short way from the stop. It was a house built of *plythari*[5], a brick made from clay and straw, a technique that must have somehow been handed down from the time of the Pharaohs in Egypt. The white washed house had belonged to my grandfather and his first wife. When she had passed away, my grandfather eventually remarried and continued to live in the same house with his new wife, my grandmother Kyriaki.

As we approached the house, we could see Grandmother waiting for us in the shade of the pomegranate tree at the entrance of her garden. She was a stout woman with round shoulders. She was dressed in a simple, plain black blouse and long village skirt. On her head she wore a black *kouroukla*[6], a light cotton kerchief that covered her hair. Her smiling face seemed weather worn but exuded an ambience of kindness. Grandmother welcomed us, welcomed us with embraces and kisses. First, she kissed Mother and then she kissed my sister and me with her special warmth. She embraced and showered us with kind kisses, with love in her eyes and gentleness in her voice.

"Welcome, my daughter, welcome, my children," she said, showing concern and affection.

"The *Panayia*[7] has helped you on your journey to me."

Nothing according to my grandmother was ever achieved without the blessing of the *Panayia*. It was her sincerest belief that no rain fell, no seed germinated, no lamb was born unless it was with the blessing of the *Panayia*. If you prayed with conviction, with honesty in your heart, with faith in your soul, she felt, you would be helped by the all-seeing, compassionate, loving Mother of God. Grandmother's faith was truly amazing.

Grandmother's embrace felt hot and damp, her kiss left the perspiration of her face on my cheek. Inside, her house felt cool, it was a relief to be out of the scorching sun; she gave us water from the huge clay urn, the pithari[8], that stood in a dark corner of the kitchen. The urn was the height of an eight-year-old child and the shape of a huge oblong ball. It felt unusually cool to the touch so that you were pleasantly surprised and wanted to embrace it to gain some relief from the heat. Its storage of water was replenished daily from the fountain outside of the village. Water was carried in smaller vessels and then emptied into the urn.

"Come and drink some water to cool you down and to bring you to your senses after all the heat that you have endured on that awful bus!" exclaimed Grandmother.

The water that she proffered to us, after our long journey, felt cold in our dry mouths and instantly refreshed us.

My mother and sister stayed for a day or two and then they had to return to Varosi. Mother tried to explain matters to me in a gentle manner.

"Mama and Kika are going to Varosi because I have to work and Kika has to go to school and there will be no one to look after you. You will have to stay with Grandmother but Mama and Kika will be back very soon to see you."

"Are you going to come tomorrow, Mama?" I asked.

"No, it will not be as soon as that. I will be here to see you after two or three weeks. Don't worry, Mama and Kika will not be very far away and Grandmother will look after you."

I could not really understand what she was trying to say and only realised the meaning when she wrapped the few things that Grandmother had prepared for her into a small bundle and then with my sister walked slowly to the bus stand at the centre of the village. The bus was already there and people were boarding.

Mother looked at me and said, "It's time for us to go, my darling, because Mama needs to go to work and there is no one to look after you in Varosi."

I then understood that Mother and Kika were going and that I was going to stay in the village with Grandmother.

"I'm going with you to Varosi, I don't want to stay here! I'm going with you!" I shouted with indignation.

Grandmother took me firmly by the shoulders and held me.

She spoke calmly but with a firm voice.

"You cannot go with Mama this time, Fotaki. Your mama has to go to work and Kika will be at school, there is no one to look after you. You have to stay here in the village for a while. It will be alright, I promise you. I will tell you lots of stories. Now, calm down," she said in a strained voice.

But I was not listening to her or anyone else. I felt that I was being abandoned, abandoned just like the time when I waited for Mother at the nursery. My heart was pounding, pounding in my chest, the blood was throbbing, throbbing in my temples, my senses were like electricity. I felt panic and an urgency to fight my way onto the bus. I wriggled out of Grandmother's grip and clutched at my mother as if I was a drowning swimmer trying to save myself. I would not let her go. I desperately held on tight to her, not wanting to be abandoned. How could she do this? I wanted to go back to Varosi with her. I suffered the extreme fear of every little child of being deserted by his or her mother. I could not bear the thought of not going with her. I clutched onto her hand. I grabbed her feet as she boarded the bus. My grandmother now tightly embraced me and called out reassuringly,

"Get on the bus quickly, both of you and leave him to me. Don't worry. I will soon calm him down."

"Look after him properly, I will be back in two weeks," my mother replied tearfully.

Meanwhile, I continued screaming while salty tears rolled down my hot cheeks.

"Mama!" I pleaded, "Don't leave me here, take me with you."

There was no consolation, there was no way out. The bus drove off leaving behind it a trail of dust carrying my mother and sister away while I remained disconsolate and inconsolable. After they had gone, I refused to go back to the house until I was eventually enticed by Grandmother's reassuring words.

For the rest of the day, I followed Grandmother around the house, into the yard and back again while she continued reassuring me that Mama would soon be back again.

"Mama is coming back very soon and she will bring you lots of sweets. If you are a good boy, you will also have a very lovely toy."

I stopped crying soon and when it was time for bed, Grandmother told me another of her magical stories about princes and princesses who had lived in far off lands long, long ago. Her therapeutic stories had a calming effect and I was soon asleep at the end of what had been a difficult day not only for me but also for my grandmother, who had soothed me with kind words, patience, love and fabulous stories.

1. hoi polloi – In Greek, the many.
2. Varosi – The modern town of Famagusta that had spread outside the Venetian walls of the old town and was mostly inhabited by Greek Cypriots until they were forced to abandon it during the 1974 Turkish invasion. Varosi is today a 'ghost town'. Its Greek Cypriot citizens are prevented from returning to their homes by the Turkish Occupation forces. The Turkish Cypriots live in the old town of Famagusta inside the Venetian walls.
3. Venetian walls – The walls of the city of Famagusta were originally built by the Lusignans. The Venetians later strengthened them and added further fortifications. In the 1571 Ottoman siege, the walls were neither breached nor captured. It was disease and starvation that forced the defenders to surrender.

A History of Cyprus. Volume 4. Sir George Bell.

4. Stylloi village – Stylloi is on the old road from Famagusta to Nicosia that stretches across the Mesaoria plain. It was a mixed village of both Greek and Turkish Cypriots who enjoyed brotherly relationships until the ethnic violence of the late 1950s and early 1960s. The village was abandoned by its Greek Cypriot inhabitants during the Turkish invasion of 1974.

5. Plythari – This is a type of brick made from mud mixed with straw then baked in the sun. This process caused the brick to harden so that it became durable even in wet weather. The houses built from plythari would be cool in the summer and retained heat during cold weather. It could also be resistant to earthquakes. This form of building was common from Neolithic times.

A History of Cyprus. Volume 1. Sir George Bell.

6. *Kouroukla* – A light cotton or linen kerchief worn by women for modesty and for protection from the sun. A black *kouroukla* indicated that a woman had been widowed.

7. The *Panayia* – The Virgin Mary, Mother of God. She is highly venerated by Greeks who often pray to her, particularly during times of personal or national crises.

'Panagia' is very deep in the Greek psyche. A Greek may hastily mutter 'My Panagia', requesting instant help if he or she finds himself or herself suddenly in danger. This is an instant appeal for protection from the forces which are beyond control. If the danger is not imminent, the Greek may whisper, "Panagia, extend your arm."

Actes du XXX11 Congress d'Historie de la Medicine. Eric Fierens. 1991. Page 156.

8. Pithari – A large, clay urn used for the storage of water or wine. In use since ancient times.

Grandmother

Grandmother's simple home was a hive of activity and a hubbub of noise. It was a traditional Cyprus house of the type that was most common in the villages before the 1950s. It was on one level in the shape of a rectangle divided into three parts. The middle section had the front and back entrances. This served as a sitting area and usually had a table and chairs; it is where guests were received and where the family sat during their time together. On the walls were some family photographs that showed men dressed in the *vraka* trousers and women with hair tied back in the *kouroukla*. During the hot summer, both front and back doors remained open to allow any breeze to cool the house. On the right was the kitchen where food was stored. There were sacks of grain, potatoes and large, round clay jars in which the halloumi goat cheese was kept in a mixture of salty water sprinkled with mint. To the left was the bedroom with an iron bed and the *armary*, a huge wardrobe made from hard wood that was decorated with hand carved patterns around the edges and was fitted with a strong iron lock, so that the family valuables could be safely deposited. People, depending on their financial means, could add further rooms to the original design.

My aunties regularly visited the house, bringing their children, my cousins, with them. There was often a flock of children who ran from the house into the yard and back. They talked and argued, they played and fought, they laughed and cried. There were no dull moments and there was no boredom.

Grandmother was the seamstress of the village and was constantly measuring, cutting, fitting and making dresses. Her Singer sewing machine was driven by a foot pedal and it was a valuable and prized possession because it enabled her to earn enough money for the family. It gave her a sense of importance; for she, unlike most other women in the village, had a craft, a profession that gave her a sense of worth. Apart from making dresses, she was also very busy cleaning, cooking and looking after the children. And how she seemed to love it! Her grandchildren, like little chicks, gathered around her. She never shouted at them or became angry if they did anything wrong. Her patience was enduring, even saintly.

She smiled, encouraged, joked and gently directed her grandchildren on how to behave when they argued amongst themselves. She showered them with a warm ambience and adoration and they, in return, showed their love by following her everywhere she went, constantly calling with up-raised faces and persistent demands for her attention.

"*Yiayia! Yiayia! Yiayia!*"[1]

But when Grandfather came home in the evening, all the noise ceased. Everything became hushed and subdued. The children stopped running around. The friends and neighbours sensed that it was time to go home. They quickly wished us goodnight and with their departure, peace, quiet and tranquillity descended upon the house. The only sound that could be heard was the noise from Grandmother's footsteps as she shuffled around the kitchen, getting ready our evening meal. She prepared the supper which was usually fried potatoes mixed with eggs and onions. Sometimes she boiled beans with potatoes that were sprinkled with olive oil, lemon and salt. There was always lots of bread that Grandmother baked once a week in the *fournos*, the earthen oven that was in her garden at the back of the house. The plates of food were put on a paneri[2] that was placed on a stool. We ate in silence and in awe of our brooding grandfather.

Grandmother was a great storyteller. She could tell stories in a marvellous and unforgettable manner. I looked forward to the storytelling hour with great relish. Apart from playing out with the other village children, I liked nothing better than the stories that my grandmother told. She would lie in the middle of her high iron bed like some elderly Scheherazade[3] with my sister Kika, whenever she was in the village, on one side and with me on the other. She always waited for us to ask. My sister with surprising confidence always spoke first.

"Tell us a story, Grandmother, please," she said.

"Yes, tell us a story," I pleaded.

She waited until everything was still and silent. From either side, we looked up at her smiling, gentle face, feeling her warmth and absolute love. Then she began…

"This story is called 'The Little Beetle' (*Koutsoukoutou*[4])." I became very excited because I'd heard it before and it was one of my favourite stories. Kika and I both clapped our hands and loudly exclaimed our satisfaction.

"Be quiet or you will wake your grandfather and he will be angry," she said in a whisper so that we would not feel as if she was displeased with us in any way.

So, when we had stopped fidgeting, she began in her very special storytelling voice:

23

"Once upon a time…" And at the sound of these words, I was transported to the magical world of talking animals, giants, monsters and fairies… "There lived a little beetle who had made up her mind to find a husband. But because she lacked grace and beauty, her concern was that she would not succeed in finding a rich and handsome man. In her favour, however, the little Koutsoukoutou had an unusual amount of intelligence and was able to make a pretty good plan. She went off to the flour mill. She crept in unseen amongst the many sacks of flour that were piled up high in the store room of the mill. In there, she took a handful of the fine, powdery flour and rubbed it on her face like a rich lady would use expensive cosmetics. When she had finished, she imagined herself to have become very beautiful and so, with great pride and confidence, she set off to make her dream come true."

At this point, Grandmother paused and looked down at us to see if we were awake or asleep. Kika and I were wide awake, in suspense and spellbound with her telling of the story. Would the little Koutsoukoutou, we asked ourselves, be successful in her quest to find a rich and handsome husband? Grandmother resumed her story.

"The little Koutsoukoutou walked on for a long time until she met a rich merchant leading a caravan of camels loaded with an abundance of merchandise that he intended to trade in a far-off town. As soon as he caught sight of the Koutsokoutou, he began to boldly address her:

'Where are you going, my pretty lady, unaccompanied, on a lonely road like this?' he said this with a smile on his face.

'I am searching for a worthy man to marry, my dear sir,' she answered, feeling rather proud of her self.

The merchant who was the kind of man who would always see an opportunity in all kinds of unlikely circumstances thought for a moment and then made his proposal.

'Why don't you marry me?' he said with a sparkle in his eye.

'Impossible, I want my life to be worth something,' she answered with some disdain.

'Why, will you waste it with me?' he answered in surprise. 'I will give you a fine house, servants and all the wonderful things that money can buy. You will live like a queen!'

The Koutsoukoutou couldn't help but be tempted by such a wonderful proposal. Apart from the wealth he had, the merchant was also quite a handsome fellow. So, the Koutsoukoutou decided to ask him a testing question.

'And sometimes, my dear sir, if we argue like all married couples sometimes do, will you beat me with the wooden rod that you use for prodding your camels with?' she asked her question with anticipation in her look and voice.

The merchant knew from experience that in a business transaction there must be negotiation for the best deal to be achieved and so he was careful and measured in his response.

'I am not a hard man,' he said with a cunning smile. 'At most, I will give you no more than a couple of strokes and that will be when I'm really angry,' he added, feeling rather pleased with his generosity of spirit."

My grandmother paused and laughed at this.

"Why, I don't think he is being very kind or generous!" she exclaimed. "Let us see how the Koutsoukoutou will answer him."

She resumed her story, speaking it as if she was reading from a classic book of children's fairy tales.

"As soon as Koutsoukoutou heard this, she knew that the rich merchant was not for her. Without much ado, she excused herself.

'I'm terribly sorry, my dear sir, but I'm in a great hurry,' and without looking at him for a second longer, she walked off, leaving the merchant standing there with all his camels and rich merchandise, feeling confused and wondering what he had said wrong."

My sister and I were now in suspense. What would happen to the brave little Koutsoukoutou? What would be the outcome of her quest? Would she succeed or would she fail? We wanted to know and we determined not to tolerate a suspension of the story before its conclusion.

"Grandmother, don't stop!" I exclaimed loudly, forgetting that poor, old Grandfather was trying to sleep in the adjoining room.

"Go on, Grandmother, otherwise we won't be able to close our eyes tonight," added my sister, who was even more eager than me to hear the rest of the story. So, Grandmother resumed her narration:

"The Koutsoukoutou walked on and on until by chance, she saw a ploughman who was driving a pair of cows to plough his nearby field. When the Koutsoukoutou came close to him, he greeted her in a friendly manner and inquired why she was travelling alone on the road. She gave the same answer to him as she gave to the merchant.

'I am searching for a man worthy to be my husband,' she replied with a sense of pride.

Without any hesitation and feeling as if this was his lucky day, the ploughman made an immediate proposal, promising that she would always have fresh produce of the land and all the milk and cheese that her appetite could desire for her breakfast and supper. The Koutsoukoutou, on hearing these promises, blushed a little because she quite liked the ploughman. He appeared to be a big handsome fellow with a thick moustache and a very convincing smile. She therefore decided to ask him

25

the test question. This time, she thought, she would try to be a little diplomatic. She wanted to draw the right answer from him so that she could successfully conclude her search and finally find happiness.

'My dear sir, it is so charming of you to make me such an offer, but I have a simple question to ask you before I can make reply. Tell me, dear sir, as you know it is a common thing for even the most loving of couples to sometimes argue and to become angry with each other, but they always find a way to deal with such problems. Tell me, dear sir, how would you deal with me if we were married and on occasion argued with one another?' The Koutsoukoutou waited in anticipation for the handsome ploughman to answer.

'I will naturally beat you with my stick and that will be the end of the arguments,' he said, believing that a man should show that he is the master of the house and that the wife would appreciate such decisiveness.

On hearing this answer, the Koutsoukoutou took fright. The ploughman was not to her liking and she hurried off along the road without looking back at him even to say goodbye. He was left standing by the road side with his two cows, feeling perplexed, confused and surprised because he could not understand why the Koutsoukoutou had decided to leave so suddenly and in such a hurry.

After a while, the Koutsoukoutou slowed her pace and began to feel a little more relaxed. The ploughman had been left far behind and could no longer be a distraction or waste her time. As she walked on, she began to notice the beauty of the countryside. The air was full of the symphony of birds making melodies that gently flouted across the countryside. The fields were like a green carpet decorated with flowers of many colours. There were purple and red, yellow and white flowers. Their aroma was intoxicating, so that quite unexpectedly, the Koutsoukoutou felt so inspired by nature and with overwhelming feelings that her future husband might be found sooner rather than later, she began to sing:

'The gentle soul that I shall marry,
to far off holidays he will carry,
me, to love and kiss,
and to live in bliss.
Who wants a husband to be a brute,
to scream, shout and to be rude?
I want a husband full of charm,
Who will never do me harm,
bold and strong,
and who will never do me wrong[5]...'

Just then, quite by chance, she came across a little grey mouse. When the mouse saw her, he enquired of her:

'Where are you journeying, my lady?'

'I'm on my way to find a husband,' she answered, not feeling terribly impressed by the little mouse.

'But why go on searching? Why don't you marry me?' he spoke with charm and confidence. He smiled in a warm manner and bowed to her like a true gentleman that seeks to impress a lady.

When the Koutsoukoutou observed his delightful manners, she felt pleased with the proposal but nevertheless, she had the usual question ready.

'If we are married and you become angry with me for some reason or other, how will you deal with me?'

The little mouse was cleverer than the previous suitors of the Koutsoukoutou. He understood immediately what was in her heart and mind. He could read between the lines. The reason for her question was clear and simple. He wanted to reassure her, he wanted to make her laugh and to feel comfortable. Most of all he wanted to pass the test.

'Why, my dear, I will certainly beat you softly with my tail,' he answered with a kind smile on his face.

The Koutsoukoutou understood that this was the man, or should I say, the mouse for her. Unreservedly, unhesitatingly, uninhibitedly, she immediately and happily agreed to the proposal.

The date was set, and the invitations were sent to family and friends. On the day of the wedding, all the guests gathered together to celebrate the happy occasion. There were birds and bunnies, squirrels and sheep, hounds and humans; anybody who was somebody came to join in the celebration. Even the merchant and the ploughman, despite their great disappointment in failing to win the Koutsoukoutou's hand in marriage, were present to offer their best wishes and congratulations to the happy couple.

The party was soon in full swing. The sun was shining and the guests were dancing. Soon, all the water had been drunk and everyone began to feel rather thirsty. The bride, who really wanted to please all her guests, quickly grabbed the clay water jugs and walked in the direction of the fountain.

Poor Koutsoukoutou! It had been a very long day for her.

The excitement, the joy and all the festivities had left her feeling tired and so she decided to sit down and have a little rest just for five minutes to catch her breath. Being so exhausted, she unwillingly fell into a deep sleep.

Meanwhile the bridegroom and guests had noticed that the bride had been gone for a while now, they were becoming anxious. Where could she be? The bridegroom was now very decisive. He immediately set off in search of her. He hadn't walked too far when he saw her sleeping soundly on the soft grass. He became so angry! He lifted his tail up high, as high as it could go and with it he began to smite the sleeping Koutsoukoutou.

The Koutsoukoutou awoke in a panic and tried to protect herself from the blows she was receiving but immediately realised that the blows she was receiving tickled her. She was tickled so much by the little mouse's tail that she began to laugh. She laughed so much that the anger left the mouse and he joined in the laughter with her. Great was their joy, great was their laughter and great was their satisfaction! The birds continued their melodies, the air was full of the rich aroma of flowers and a gentle breeze refreshed the loving couple. In due course, arm in arm, kissing and embracing, they picked up the jugs, filled them with water and carried them back to the wedding feast where they continued to dance and laugh… And you, my, my dears, have laughed even more than them."

Grandmother's tone always expressed the magical or mysterious quality of the story; her telling of the story became rhythmic so that it had a momentum that evolved as it was spoken. It always gripped our attention. We felt the suspense in our hearts as the stories of handsome princes and beautiful princesses, witches and goblins, mermaids and of fantastic sea voyages to magical far off lands unfolded to inspire our childish imaginations.

Her storytelling was a wonderful experience and my memory of that has never faded. Grandmother looked after my sister and me with her warmth and tenderness. She blessed us in her simple devout manner and prayed that we should become teachers or doctors for the benefit of mankind and who, in her estimation, were the most important people in society. Needless to say, that she above all was our great teacher whose kind words, good example, common sense and fairness taught us some pragmatic ethical thinking. Children learn through observation and through listening and we learnt from her. She shared her food with others though she only had barely enough for her own needs. She spoke kindly and comforted those who suffered loss, injustice or unfairness. She was a decent person who could be relied on and in the years to come, it is my belief that our grandmother had a great influence on our values and attitudes in life.

On the day when we were going to depart for England, she came to Varosi with Grandfather, my aunts, my uncles and cousins to bid us farewell. She was hot and flustered; her face was sad and anxious. The separation for her was a painful experience. She didn't quite understand the geography, the distances involved. For her, it may have been like travelling to another town on the island. She begged my mother not to go for she feared that my father would continue to prove unreliable. She reminded my mother that he was a gambler and a drinker.

"You know his habits and you know that he will not change."

She tried to appeal to Mother's common sense and she was very determined that Mother should not leave Cyprus.

"He will only let you down; you and the children will suffer. Who is going to come to knock on your door with help, with a kind word when you will be so far from home and so far from the arms of your family?"

Mother, however, remained determined that she should join her husband for better or for worse. For Grandmother, it was obvious that Mother was taking a very big risk because she was going to leave her relatives behind and in a new country she would not have the family support that she had hitherto enjoyed.

Grandmother was a simple village person who knew little about the world. I suppose if one was to say to her that the earth was flat and that the moon was made from cheese, she would not have questioned it because such matters had never been made relevant to her through a process of normal, basic education. For her, the whole planet consisted of Cyprus and a few other familiar countries that she had heard of when people spoke about the wider world. She was typical of many women of her generation in Cyprus who worked extremely hard, bore children but who were never given the opportunity to discover anything about the world. Grandmother's lack of education was balanced by the great love that she had for her family. Her simple understanding of geography and her great love is exemplified in the following story.

She had never heard of the town of Aberfan in Wales. Well, when Mother, my sister and I had been in England for some time, a terrible tragedy struck the people of the small coalmining town of Aberfan. Aberfan was surrounded by coal slag heaps from the local mines. Tragically, heavy rain caused movement in the mounds; on 21st October, 1966, there was a landslide that sent thousands of tonnes of coal slag on to the nearby houses and a junior school that stood in the way of the torrent. The time was just after 9 am in the morning when it happened. It was a terrible accident in which 130 people died – mainly school children and their teachers who were buried alive.[6]

The news of this very sad event travelled fast even to Stylloi in Cyprus where Grandmother immediately began to mourn the death of my sister and me. She was a simple soul who loved much but who had very little understanding of the world beyond her village. She imagined that in England, where we had gone to, there was only one school just like in

Stylloi and that my sister and I were amongst the children of the school who had lost their lives when the mud had submerged the school. She was reassured by those around her that Aberfan was far away from London where we lived, but she was not convinced until a letter arrived from my mother and father, informing her that we were not involved in the tragic accident that had befallen the unfortunate people of Aberfan.

In the letter, Father tried to explain that England was not a big village but that it was a big country that had many great cities, much greater and much bigger than even Nicosia and that it had thousands of towns and villages of which Aberfan was only one. It was as if he was trying to explain something to a little child who needed everything to be expressed in very simple terms. He did not mention that Aberfan is a place in Wales because he had no wish to confuse his distraught mother-in-law any further. By a gradual process, Grandmother was made to understand that my sister and I were safe and sound.

1. Yiayia – Greek for grandmother.
2. Paneri – This was made from straw tightly woven together into the shape of a round board approximately the size of a small table top and when placed on a flat surface such as a stool, it could function as a small table. It was often decorated in traditional folk patterns. After use, it could be hung on the wall as an ornament.
3. Sheherazade – She is the heroine storyteller in the tales of *One Thousand and One Arabian Nights*. The Sultan who has been disappointed in marriage is determined to avenge himself by taking a bride every day and then executing her the morning after the wedding night. Sheherazade, however, on the night of her wedding, cleverly entertains the Sultan with a story that she does not complete by morning when she is due to be executed. The Sultan is so keen to hear the end of the story that he spares her life for that day. The next night Sheherazade repeats the same rouse until eventually the Sultan recognises her special qualities, falls in love with her and they live, as the story goes, happily ever after.
4. Koutsoukoutou – This is a well-known and much loved traditional Cyprus folk tale. Its details illustrate the pastoral life of the people. The essence of the story isn't about finding romantic love, but rather it is about the search for a husband who will show respect and consideration. There are different versions of the story, some of which emphasise that the Koutsoukoutou is unable to find a husband because she is black and in order to overcome what she sees as a problem, she visits the flour mill where she applies the flour to her body to cover her blackness. This aspect of the story

in which black or dark skin is associated with ugliness is to be condemned and rejected. EACEA. E Koutsoukoutou (To Skatharaki).

5. The Aberfan Disaster – This tragedy was widely reported on radio, television and in the newspapers. The headlines on the front page of 'The Times' on the 22nd October, 1966 were: 200 FEARED DEAD AFTER SLAG BURIES SCHOOL.

From Stylloi to Sotira

Grandfather left home before sunrise and returned after dark. My grandmother served his food and he ate in silence and in silence we would all sit around, watching him. He had down cast eyes and a long moustache with dropping ends. He was old even then and his sturdy frame filled the doorway. He was like some hero out of Homer's epics. His wife and daughters were respectful and obedient towards him. I now realise that perhaps they feared him somewhat, for he had a terrible temper. He was at least six feet in height; he had dark eyes and straight grey hair that lay flat over his forehead. His hands were large and heavy, the skin was worn and farrowed like old leather and permanently ingrained by the heat of the sun and the hours of hard labour upon the land. He wore high boots and carried a *matsouka*, a shepherd's staff made from the enduring wood of the olive tree. He was a master shepherd who herded sheep from dawn to dusk.

Frixos, his dog, was always never far from him. He had smooth black hair on his back and long yellow hair on his underbelly. He was a large, impressive dog, more like a wolf than a sheep dog. He was loveable towards familiar people but hostile towards strangers, at whom he snarled until Grandfather would call him to heel. He was a diligent and hardworking dog, eager to please his owner. In the fields, master and dog worked like a team. Grandfather whistled instructions that sent the dog to harry the sheep to the right or to the left. Sometimes, when a sheep strayed from the flock, Frixos ran at it, he barked and growled, he blocked its path, turned it around and then speedily chased it back to reunite with the flock. Grandfather loved his dog like a true friend.

One day, when Grandfather had come home from tending the sheep, Grandmother prepared the evening meal and put it on the *paneri*. Grandfather was exhausted from wandering in the fields with his sheep all day long under the hot sun. He washed his hands in a bowl of water, then sat down to have his supper. No sooner had he sat down to eat when the cat that had been sleeping in the corner of the room smelt the food, sauntered lazily over to where we were sitting and hopped onto the *paneri*. As fast as lightening Grandfather grabbed the cat and threw it hard upon the wall. He cursed and blasphemed like a madman. The cat screeched and ran out with its hair on end. His anger ceased and he sat down again, quiet and composed, while we continued to look on, not daring to utter a word to him. His cruel treatment of the cat was in contrast to his feelings for his dog. Grandfather had an air of mystery about him. He was a man of few words, a guardian of secrets, as it turned out. Many years after, during a casual conversation, my sister revealed some family matters relating to Grandfather.

"Oh, didn't you know that Grandfather's mother was Turkish?" she asked. "And her name was Fatima[1]. You see, it was a matter of the heart. His father was called George and he was a hired shepherd for a rich Turkish Cypriot landowner in Trikomo. As it happened, George, our great-grandfather somehow met with Fatima and they both fell in love with each other."

I listened with utter interest as my sister continued to reveal the love story.

"Well, love doesn't recognise if you are Greek or Turk. Race, being a Christian or a Moslem doesn't mean a thing when you are in love. The two conspired and ran away together. Despite the threats and counter threats from the families, Fatima was baptised and became Christina and she married our great-grandfather, George. Would it have mattered if George had become Hassan or Mehmet for the sake of his love? Are we not just the same people?" my sister asked philosophically, then paused for a moment before she resumed her tale. "It was a real *Romeo and Juliet* story with a happy ending." She then added as an afterthought, "Perhaps Cyprus might have been a much happier place if more people had followed their example."

This was a revelation to me. We had always been so proud of our Hellenic identity and suddenly we were not entirely what we thought we were. Now, we live in a time and place when we can accept mixed marriages, but I can only have great sympathy for my great-grandfather and great-grandmother, who disregarded all conventions dividing the two communities of Cyprus for the sake of their love. They were like two heroic characters in some romantic novel or film who would not allow anything to prevent them from fulfilling their love. They must have had unbelievable courage and belief in each other to challenge the powerful and entrenched rules of their society.

This family story certainly prompted me to examine my feelings towards the 'so-called' historic enemies of the Greek people. As a child, I had been subjected to my fair share of anti-Turkism through my exposure to the standard educational issues of reading books from the Greek Ministry of Education that were also available to Greek Cypriot children living in England. These books presented the Turks as a barbaric horde intent on destroying Greek Christian civilisation. The psychological effect on children was severe. It was as if Attila the Hun had never died and was about to attack and lay waste to civilisation. Such propaganda inspired fear, hate and the desire for revenge. Another influence that had contaminated my view of Turks and presented them as thieves, rapists and cold-blooded killers was the Greek press whose newspapers were widely available in the Greek Cypriot cafés and shops in London. I am certain that the Turkish Ministry of Education and the Turkish press were doing an equally thorough job in teaching the Turkish people about how the Greek Army had invaded Anatolia in 1920 and committed heinous crimes against the Turkish Nation and that all Greek Cypriots wanted to murder the Turkish Cypriots and proclaim union with Greece.

Of course, nationalist propaganda works effectively if it can appeal to our fears and insecurities. It works particularly well on the young and those unable to think critically. It is my belief that for over a long period of time, the peoples of Greece, Turkey and Cyprus have been subjected to the type of nationalism that has led to extreme attitudes and even blind hatred between the citizens of these countries. Matters became and continue to be even more complex in Cyprus where both ethnicities are present.

The discovery that my great-grandmother was a Turkish Cypriot should not have surprised me because it is pretty obvious that there has been intermingling between the two peoples in Cyprus despite the conventions that prevented Moslems and Christians from marrying. In fact, recent scientific evidence[2] has strongly supported what Cypriots have always understood about themselves but have chosen to ignore – that the Greek Cypriots and Turkish Cypriots have a common ancestry and what links them is not only the habitation of the same island but also the same blood line. Unfortunately, the Cypriots, like the Capulets and the Montaques in Shakespeare's tragedy of feuding families in Verona, have not been perceptive enough to notice the many wonderful things which could unite them: love for their common homeland, the value of family life and aspirations for their children, also the work ethic that often drives them to labour for long hours, doing two or three jobs every day. Most of all, there is also the natural friendship and fondness that Cypriots had for each other, that was interrupted, suppressed, overturned and disowned with the rise of nationalism and the dirty politics that followed. And now, we also have the evidence from the scientists who present us with the real facts relating to our identity. The small differences were emphasised and these have been used as an excuse for hate and division. The Greek and Turkish Cypriots, like the Montaques and the Capulets, who suffer the loss of their children, remain on the verge of a similar tragedy. At least for our family, there was in this instance a happy ending; the romance of our great grandparents resulted in a fruitful marriage with the birth of numerous children and grandchildren. There were many such stories in Cyprus which were hushed up with the gathering nationalistic storm that devastated the island from about the mid-1950s, culminating in its partition in 1974. I sometimes reflect upon this sad story of war, suffering and division and ask when will the Greeks and Turks cease to be prisoners of their history and finally accept that they are linked by the ties of history, culture and blood? When will they realise that the drama doesn't have to conclude as a tragedy in which everybody suffers but rather, in a wonderful synthesis of two peoples who have so much in common?

~

As a child, Mother was a shepherdess, tending flocks of sheep with her father on the wide plain of Mesaoria, that in spring time, exploded into colour. Grey clouds swept in by Borias, the north wind, rolled over the Pentathaktilos Mountains, gathering low over Mesaoria where they shed their water content on to the plain. The heavy rain turned the dry and dusty earth into a carpet of deep green grass, speckled with the yellow and white narcissus. Pedias and Lalias, the rivers of Mesaoria, that had dried up during the summer months filled and flowed yet again with cool, clean fresh water. Sometimes their banks burst, quenching the thirst of the dry soil that for a few weeks became a rich tapestry of flowers, as if woven in fine silk. Oregano and thyme, basil and rosemary, sage and saffron grew in rich abundance on the banks of the rivers and streams, exuding powerful aromas of herb and spice. Mesaoria, the place between the mountains, was full of hard working country people tending their flocks in the busy season of lambing or where sunburnt men expertly guided their horse drawn ploughs, clicking at the horses, cutting long straight farrows into the rich soil, preparing their fields for the sowing of seed while inwardly praying for the success of the crop so that children, wives and elderly parents would not hunger during the coming winter.

Like the blossom of the lemon tree, the spring does not endure for very long in Cyprus. The heat of summer rushes in with vengeful, severe and burning intensity.

In Mesaoria, my mother spent her childhood years with her father, helping to tend flocks of sheep. It wasn't easy to awake in the early hours of the morning before the sun had even glimpsed over the horizon, when sleep for a child is physically nourishing and so sweet but Mother as a child awoke promptly, without complaint and she did this day after day of her childhood. They dressed and put their provisions for the day into the shoulder bag, the vourka, made from the skin of a sheep and decorated with tussles and coloured stones. Grandfather, his little daughter and his dog Frixos then walked to the outskirts of the village to where the sheep fold was situated. The dog, with some loud barking and throaty growling, quickly roused the sheep and they were led out of the gate of the stone built fold, walking under the star speckled night sky, towards the open fields and grassland of the Mesaoria Plain while their rusty iron sheep bells were jangling and clanging, breaking the silent stillness of the early morning. From before dawn until after dusk, winter or summer, my grandfather and his little daughter trekked across the plain, grazing their sheep.

Not everything was as happy as it might have appeared. Mother knew that while she tended sheep, even though the stars shone brightly over Mesaoria or that the flowers of the fields were beautiful to behold, many other children of the village went to school but she did not. The carpet of white and purple anemones, the crowds of yellow and pink daises and the host of plum red poppies could not take away the hurt that she felt at the thought that while her peers had the privilege to go to school, she was excluded. Why should she not join the other children whom, on occasion, she had seen dancing and singing, hand in hand, every morning on their way to school? Why should she not learn how to read and write with them? Why should she grow up an uneducated person? These thoughts were constantly on her mind. One day, she summoned the courage to ask,

"Father, when shall I go to school?"

The older she became, the more often she asked this question and Grandfather avoided giving her an answer. He would move on as if to tend the flock, whistling commands to Frixos, his dog, and calling out to the sheep.

On one rare occasion Grandfather looked at his little daughter and attempted to answer the question that she constantly asked. He did not often engage in conversation with others nor was he a man who showed any eagerness to express his ideas. He always preferred to keep his thoughts to himself as if he was reluctant to trust those around him or perhaps he remained silent because he could not give a pleasing answer to his young inquisitor. On this occasion, his little daughter's direct and courageous challenge made him feel that he was obliged to at least try to explain something about the injustice of life that made it difficult for a little girl, who wanted to learn how to read and write, to attend school.

"Andriani," he began his answer to the question slowly and deliberately, pausing to think carefully about his choice of words.

"Andriani, you know that I was never sent to school by my father, and to this day, I do not know how to read and write and neither did my father before me. I know that not being able to read and write is like being blind because we cannot understand much of what is in God's creation. My destiny was to be a shepherd and there was nothing that I could do to change it."

"Father," she continued to argue, "just because you were unfortunate and didn't go to school, must I share the same fate? It isn't fair! In school I can learn, Father. I can begin to become something more than a person who doesn't know anything about the world. I know that school will help me to become something wonderful in this life. My godsisters are going to school and they are already reading. I sometimes go to their house and they allow me to sit with them while they are reading from their books. It is a wonderful thing to learn letters, to read and to write. Why am I here in the fields, looking after sheep from morning until dusk? Why am I not at school with the other children? What will I ever learn looking after sheep day after day?"

Grandfather was perplexed and hardly knew how to respond to this outpouring from his little daughter. He knew she was right, he knew she was justified and he understood her frustration. He was a father, and of course, he wanted to help his child, but how? How was he ever going to send her to school when he didn't have two rials in his pocket and when providing food for the family was the most imperative need.

"Do you think, Andriani, that I have the means to send you to school but for some selfish reason I refuse? No, you are quite mistaken. Kanikli, your godfather, is the richest man in the village. He has more land and more herds of animals than any other man in this area. He has the money to send your godsisters to school. In comparison to him, we have very little. He has money, that is why his daughters go to school and we are poor, that is why your help is needed for the sustenance of our family. That is why you are not at school."

He abruptly stopped speaking; he looked down at the earth as if in troubled thought then looked again at his little daughter who continued to have an apprehensive and troubled expression on her face.

"Who knows?" he said. "Only Almighty God knows the future. One day, perhaps, you will go to school."

Andriani understood that there was a season and a time for all things. The sunrise and the sunset, winter and summer, sowing and harvest. These were the cycles and the rhythms of life. She also knew that there was a time for children to go to school but this would not happen for her.

Her father looked sadly at her. He gave her a rare and encouraging smile and then they continued their walk across the fields in the midst of white and purple flowers and where the air was intoxicating with the smell of oregano and lavender. They walked on, saying very little, leading their sheep on to fresh pastures.

~

I know that school was important to Mother because as an adult, she often spoke about it. During the 1920s, there was a great deal of poverty in Cyprus and it seemed more useful for a child, particularly for a girl to help her parents with work in the fields, gathering in the harvest or looking after the sheep of a rich landowner to earn a few rials for the needs of the family. It seemed however, that my mother's question about going to school weighed heavily on the mind of her father. He had struck a bargain with the village school teacher for my mother to attend school and in return, my mother cleaned the teacher's house. She earned two or three rials and with this money she bought the books that she needed for her lessons.

My mother was delighted and was able to briefly attend the village school for a very short period of time. Not being able to carry on must have been a great disappointment to her, but her help was needed to earn a little more money for the support of the family. This was the sad reality for most Cypriots at that time. If you were a landowner or a member of the professional classes, those who had some wealth, then you were able to educate your children. If you were poor, then your children did not have the opportunity to get much of an education. Equality of opportunity had not yet been born.

~

Though education was entirely free in England, it was not so in Cyprus that had been annexed by the British in 1914 and had formally become a crown colony in 1925. In Cyprus, poor families had to buy their books for primary school and secondary education was beyond the reach of the vast majority of Cypriots. So, without books, it was difficult for my mother to continue with even the basics of reading and writing. In this day and age, it seems awful that a child should be desperate to learn, should hunger for an education and to be deprived of the opportunity because of the lack of a few pennies that would pay for books. Mother was deprived but she always retained her desire to learn. I can clearly remember how, as an adult, she cared for her family, worked from morning until night and at the same time struggled to teach herself reading and writing. She often, with great concentration, tried to decipher a text, reading and rereading each word slowly and carefully. She began to read individual words and then sentences and whole pages and, eventually, she read whole books. She showed the capacity to learn and often said to us with a smile on her face and a voice full of emotion,

"If I had had the opportunities that you young people have today, I would have become something marvellous!"

Looking back, I think that it was no idle boast; she would certainly have achieved something stunning.

Her parents named her Andriani and it was a name entirely suitable for her because it means manly strength. I know that her life experiences often required an enormous amount of spiritual and psychological endurance for her to survive. A real test of her strength was her marriage, because though Father was a kind and loving man, he could sometimes be irresponsible. It seems that when she married him, his family felt that Mother was not an appropriate match. They considered themselves a rich family of landowners from Sotira while she was only a daughter of a shepherd from Stylloi. Looking back on their lives together, his marriage to Mother was probably the best thing that he ever did! But his family did not realise it at the time.

When my parents married in 1942, they lived in Sotira for some time and this is where my sister Kika was born in November 1943. Father had a shoe maker's shop. He was a skilled craftsman, able to measure, cut and hand stitch shoes and boots of every description. He often told the story with a sparkle in his eye about how he cycled to Paralimni from Sotira to learn his trade from a maestro who was reluctant to teach him.

"I went to the work shop day after day," my father would say, "and this mean person made me spend hours on dyeing the leather instead of showing me the techniques of cutting and stitching. I had worked at the shop for a whole year before I was allowed to measure a customer for shoes. He did not want me to learn, he was afraid that I might have become more skilful then him and take his customers. So, do you know what I did?"

He would pause and smile at his own cunning.

"Whenever the maestro was working on a special pair of shoes that needed some delicate technique, I pretended to be busy somewhere close to him so that I could observe his methods. It wasn't the best way to learn but he forced me to become a thief of his craft because he did not want to teach me anything. I served a seven-year apprenticeship and I learnt more than he was willingly to teach me."

The end of his story was always followed by a hearty laughter. In a more serious tone, he always added an epilogue to his tale.

"In those days, I was one of the more promising young men in the village. I was a master of a trade. I had my own shop. I owned a fine bicycle made in Sheffield and my family were wealthy and well established. My mother, your grandmother, had already spoken to me, my brother and my sister about our inheritance. I could look ahead to making a good life for myself…but then, things went terribly wrong."

At this serious point in the story, he smiled gently and changed the subject. Mother filled the gaps in the story. Their time in the village was far from the idyllic life. Father was bad tempered, often cursing and shouting, and at this time, he became involved in a political adventure to raid the British Military Base of Acrotiri; the plan was to capture some barrels of oil. Father said that this was resistance against the British. The plan failed, and Father was even wounded as the raiders tried to escape. As a child, I often noticed the scar of the flesh wound on his right shoulder.

It was prison for him and the other freedom fighters. When he returned after the war, Mother's life with him did not improve because prison seemed to have made him a less caring person. He sold what he had and wasted the money. They were left penniless. Even after many years, Mother sometimes still became distressed speaking about this period in her life. Her depression was so great that while pregnant, she felt such anguish that she aborted her pregnancy. She saw no future and no hope. It was difficult to care for one child. Kika, my sister was about three or four years old. But to have another mouth to feed at a time of poverty, unemployment and an unreliable husband made matters impossible.

My sister and I were the only two people that Mother ever spoke to about this period in her life and she did this when we were mature adults. She only spoke of those sad events if the subject of the conversation happened to stray onto how difficult life was during the war years and their aftermath. She always seemed a happy and optimistic individual but when speaking about the events of this time, her countenance changed; her eyes filled with sorrow and her face suddenly aged beyond its years.

"This was the blackest period of my life," she began and as she spoke, the room that we were in became sombre and still as if in sympathetic sadness at her painful memories.

"I knew that he was sometimes foolish, but I imagined that after giving birth to you, Kika, your father would have become more settled and more responsible. He did not, and like a fool, he went from one crisis to another, dragging us along with him."

There was a hint of anger in her voice, even though the events that she described had happened long before.

"It was a terrible time for me because after he came out of prison, he seemed reckless and irresponsible. He didn't care about the consequences of his actions. It was at this time that I became pregnant again and for me, it was a sign of hope. I thought that perhaps with our second child, he would show more concern and understanding for us. His mother had given him and his brother a plot of land each next to her own house so that they could build homes for their families. The building materials were all bought and ready. In spring, the builders were due to begin the work. I hoped that all these things would make him more reasonable, more responsible. It was not to be. I was making plans for our future but unfortunately, your father had other ideas. In one mad, catastrophic week, he changed our lives forever. He sold the building materials meant for constructing our house; he took the money and went to Nicosia where he indulged himself in his vices. Then, he returned and did not tolerate one word to be spoken about this matter. Overnight, we had become without the prospect of being able to build our own home and we were penniless. I withdrew into a silent trauma, not believing the utter madness of what he had done and when in my despair, I looked at my growing womb and through the stress and worry, I lost my baby…"

She always paused at this point in the story, unable to continue, as if her heart would burst. Tears filled her dark eyes as she visually recalled this dreadful episode in her life.

"I felt that this world was very harsh and I did not want to bring another child into all this suffering."

My sister and I never questioned Mother further about the dreadful events. We understood that every now and then, she needed to repeat this story because despite the passing of the years, the wounds had not healed, nor would they ever. The retelling must have provided some momentary catharsis, it was a confession, a relief to the troubled soul, a therapy for an old wound that could never entirely heal. When she finished speaking, she wiped the tears from her face, sighed deeply and made an effort to cheer up.

"At least I have both of you my children, close to me. May God forgive me for the wrong things that I have committed in my moments of weakness," she said, trying to smile so that her sadness would not also affect us, her listeners.

Yet, like many other women in Cyprus during the 1950s, she saw no other life beyond that which she shared with her husband. It seems that for most women during this period, there was no escape from the marriage bond, even in relationships that were very destructive for them. In due course, through education and social progress, women in Cyprus steadily progressed beyond this difficulty.

The family then moved from Sotira to Stylloi, where they continued to live in dire poverty and where I was born one early morn in springtime.

I suppose Mother moved there to be nearer her own family, who at least might give her some support. Her mother and father were always at hand as well as her younger sister Eleni, who was as yet unmarried. They looked after us so that Mother could seek work either in the village, labouring in the fields or perhaps find work in Varosi. Regular work was very hard to come by, particularly in the village and travelling to Varosi from Stylloi was difficult on a daily basis. Before long, father had begun to talk about moving yet again, this time to live in Varosi, where work could be found on a more regular basis.

The early 1950s were a desperately difficult time. The world was still suffering from the trauma of war. In Cyprus, there was hardly any work; business and commerce were almost non-existent. Most people at the time lived in villages and were engaged in farming. This was not very productive because it lacked organisation and modern farming techniques. It seemed that there was a total lack of opportunities and the young families were so frustrated that they began to look towards other horizons to find work and a better future for their children.

"Why should I stay in this village," my father used to say, "to waste my time waiting for customers who never enter and not to even make enough money to buy a loaf of bread. No, I don't want this!"

1. Fatima – It is probable that Fatima was not ethnically Turkish. Her family may have been Greek Orthodox or Latin Christians who had converted to Islam. These people were called 'Linobambaki' which is translated as linen/cotton. It indicated that such people were neither Greek nor Turkish. Neither were they entirely Christian nor Moslem, neither, the one or the other, but they were something in between. Christians sometimes converted to Islam so that they could be granted rights that were only enjoyed by the ruling Moslems or even to avoid persecution. Eventually, some Linobambaki blended into the Moslem community while others reclaimed their Christian identity that they had previously hidden. In Conversion and Apostasy in the Late Ottoman Empire, Selim Deringil, Bogazici University, Cambridge University Press, 2012, page 111-112, states the following: "Anthony Bryar in the seminal study of Crypto-Christianity, was to observe that after the Crimean War, when the British and French became self-appointed guarantors of the Christian populations of the entire empire. What the Allies had not bargained for was the number of supposed Christians, supposedly registered as Muslims, who now emerged out of the woodwork to declare themselves under British and French and Russian protection[3]." The people who emerged as

secret Christians were spread over the entire Ottoman Empire and were known by a number of names, such as meso-meso, *paramesoi and dipistia in Greek; in Serbia droversto ; in Cyprus patsallosi (piebald), apostolikoi (wild carobs) or linovamvaki(linen-cottons);* in Albania laramanoi (motlcys). Bryar was to note some of their most typical characteristics '…they had double names, Christian and Muslim…they were baptised…but underwent sunnet…they had two marriages, with a Christian koumbaros and a Muslim master of ceremonies…'

2. Scientific evidence: Plos One research article analysis of Greek Cypriots reveals "Primarily common pre-Ottoman paternal ancestry with Turkish Cypriots." Published 16th June, 2016. Authors: A.Heraclides, E. Bashardes, E. Fernandez-Dominguez, S. Bertonchini, M. Chimonas, V. Christofi, T. King, Budowle, P. Manol, M.A. Cariolou.

To Varosi

There was much poverty in Cyprus during the immediate aftermath of the Second World War. There was a feeling that progress was only moving very slowly and many people were unemployed. Mother was considered fortunate to have found employment with British services families, cleaning their houses. She worked so hard for her living but she only earned pennies; for the poor it was always just for a few pennies. She cleaned two or three of their houses every day but never had enough money for our basic needs.

We had moved to Varosi by then and lived in a *baranga*, a short distance from the beach that would one day be developed into a tourist resort with luxury hotels and in turn be abandoned with the murderous onslaught of the Turkish invasion of 1974.

The *baranga* was a kind of cabin, a rectangular one room structure made from wood, corrugated iron and some bricks. I remember that our *baranga* had marble floor tiles that were broken and they had space in between the cracks so that you could see the dark earth beneath. From our *baranga,* Mother set off each morning at sunrise, marching off to work like a courageous soldier. At the end of the day, my sister and I often stood at the door of our *baranga*, peering into the night, waiting for our mother to return, to emerge from the darkness.

"When is Mama coming home, is she coming soon?" I asked my sister over and over again, fearing that I wouldn't see her again. My sister comforted me,

"Don't worry, Fotaki, Mama will soon be home, I promise you."

Eventually, Mother returned weary after the day's battle, long after the sun had gone down. She was tired, bedraggled and exhausted, but on approaching us, the tension on her expression eased and was replaced with a beaming, warm smile. First came the hugs and the kisses followed by a rush of questions: "How are you, my darlings? Are you alright? Did you have something to eat? What did you learn at school today?"

One thing for certain, we kissed her over and over again, showing our relief that she was once again home with us. It was like the sudden return of the missing soldier after the battle, to the utter delight of his loved ones.

There was no negotiation regarding how hard she had to work, because if you did not work, you would not eat. Nobody was going to help you or give some kind of assistance. Mother understood that apart from family, there was no help to be had from anywhere. Most people lived from hand to mouth and it was only the sense of family that prevented the very poor from becoming destitute and homeless. Elderly parents took in their grown-up children and their families; brothers and sisters shared what they had with each other. "Blood is thicker than water," some people often said in acknowledgement of the bonds that enabled them to survive in difficult times. Like countless other poor, working people, Mother needed money to put food on the table and counted herself very fortunate that she now had a job to go to and thanked God daily in her prayers that she had been blessed with the vigorous health and strength to work for the benefit of her children.

When I wasn't being looked after by my grandparents, my sister stayed at home to care for me, but this was at the cost of her education. Even years after my mother's childhood, children were still kept away from school to help maintain the family. The choices were difficult but had to be made.

I was then, about four or five years of age. It is the time that we begin to have a clear memory of our lives and the incidents that we can recall most clearly and which remain with us, are those that caused us most pleasure or most pain either physically or psychologically. One such event happened to me when I was about five years old and I can visualise it in my mind's eye as clearly as the day it happened:

Close to our baranga, across some parched fields and a main road along which hardly any traffic could be seen, was the beach of Varosi. The fine, golden sand stretched from the rocky outcrop below the Constantia Restaurant for two miles along the margin of the bay to Nea Salamina, founded by the heroes of Troy and which had once been the rich capital of King Evagoras who fought the Persian Empire for the liberty of Cyprus. On this dazzling beach, before the invasion and before the coming of tourism, the local children gathered to play.

I loved that time. I ran around all day long under the hot sun, dressed in only a pair of shorts, playing to my heart's content, not realising how nervous Mother was, that being a child and unaware of danger, I could be swept out to sea if the weather suddenly changed.

She often told my sister, who was only about 12 years of age, to look out for me and to never let me out of her sight. My poor sister, being frightened of the consequences threateningly articulated by Mother, became my shadow. She followed me everywhere and I made her life

45

more difficult by refusing to ever go home before Mother was due to arrive and this was often after nightfall.

Despite Mother's long hours at work, we sometimes had no food to eat and felt the pangs of hunger. Even so, we were not unhappy because we played all day long without having an adult standing over us. We tolerated and endured our hunger because we had that freedom which all children desire and value. We roamed around, played, laughed, argued, fought and then made up again. We played to our hearts content and without adults or authority to restrict us in any way. We played at our favourite haunt, the Varosi beach with its golden sand and clear blue waters. In the summer, the fine sand became so hot that the unaccustomed found it too hot to tread on, but it didn't burn us for we had developed resistance to the heat so that we could walk or run around without any discomfort. We were like young rebels. We did whatever we wanted. There was no mother, father, teacher or policeman; no rules, no one to stop us from our compulsive ecstatic play. The lack of adult supervision had led me to feel that I could take chances, but this was a mistake that my mother made me regret very soon.

One day, on the feast day of the Sotiros, The Saviour, when the *paniyiri*[1] was held in the village of Sotira, Mother planned to take us there for the day. It was still early in the morning and there were things that she needed to do. Our Aunt Eleni, Mother's younger sister, was with us.

"Mama, I want to play on the beach. Why can't I play on the beach? I want to go to the beach. My friends are at the beach. Why can't I go?"

I felt like a prisoner; it was as if I had been tied up, bound with chains. I yearned to run out, beyond my mother's control, to meet with my companions on the hot sands of the beach. This is what I had become accustomed to. I was determined and kept repeating my demands to wear her will down so that she would give in and let me go to the beach. She tried to resist.

"No, because very soon we are going to the *paniyiri*," she answered patiently.

"No, Mama, I want to go to the beach!"

She soon relented to my constant demands. Perhaps she might have been very tired from work because it was out of character for her to relent to my wishes. She had always tried and continued in the years ahead of us to maintain a firm discipline on my sister and me so that no harm might befall us. But on this occasion, she relented:

"Don't go to the rocks at the Constantia, there are deep pools. If you fall in, you will drown. Stay opposite the path from our baranga. Do you promise me not to go near the rocks?" she uttered, giving me an anxious, parental look. "And don't forget, only for a little while, then you must come home so we can get ready to go to the paniyiri."

I nodded vigorously to affirm that I understood but all I wanted to do was to get away as quickly as possible. I knew that I had got my way and I was delighted to resume my usual play. But on this occasion, my friends were nowhere to be seen. I stood on the beach like a lonely castaway, looking around for some signs of life. None of my friends were to be seen, but I was not going to be put off my determination to play, even if it was going to be without my friends.

I had a stick in my hand and having been told not to do something had the opposite effect on me: I headed straight to the far left of the beach where the rocks protruded like jagged, uneven teeth, half hidden by the sand and water.

In the centre of this outcrop, there were deep pools of a clear blue ocean decorated with white coral rock and green sea plants through which dozens of little multi-coloured fish roamed in and out. This was my favourite place on the beach and where, though forbidden to me, I often came to play solitary games in which I lost myself in some imaginary world while precariously balancing on the edge of a rock, overlooking a deep watery cavern.

Disobediently, I made my way to the edge of the pool that was surrounded by sharp coral. The pool was clear, clean and deep. There was nobody else around. Had I fallen in, I would have surely drowned.

I launched my stick into the pool and imagined that it was the ship of Odysseus. I'd recently heard the story of Odysseus and the Cyclops[2] at school and I had been thrilled by it. I was lost in the child's world of play and imagination, creating my own imaginary characters and adventures as I moved dangerously from rock to rock that overlooked the deep pool. I was immersed in Homer's world of storms and shipwrecks, escaping from cannibalistic giants, the anthropophagi[3] and the witch[4] that turned men into beasts. Odysseus was my captain and we were having a great time. We were going to help our friends escape from the cave of Polyphemos. We were going to rescue our crew that had been turned into Pig men by Kirke… Suddenly, there was an unexpected interruption. I was awoken from my daydream by a calm, quiet, firm and familiar voice.

"Fotaki…"

It was Mother. At the sound of her voice, Odysseus and his crew, one-eyed Polyphemos and his tribe of one-eyed Cyclopes quickly disappeared back into the depths of my childish imagination. My captain had abandoned me as Homer's world, vanished into thin air and I was back at the rocky pool with Mother standing a few feet away from me, trying not to show her anger. She stood there, on the burning sand, anxious and fearful of what could happen, conscious of the deep pools in the rocks on either side of me and how one small slip could lead to something unimaginable.

"Fotaki! Slowly, my child! Don't be frightened!"

I looked at her and felt her tension. I reached out to get my stick from the pool.

"Oh, be careful! Don't fall in!"

I'd managed to retrieve my stick. Then she said more quietly,

"Now, come closer towards me."

I remember that she had a very quiet voice and continued to smile strangely at me. I still felt frightened when I looked at her. Mother rarely showed any other expression other than one of tolerance and love, even when I had been a little bit naughty. On this occasion, however, I knew instinctively something wasn't right. And on that hot, mid-morning when she'd grabbed hold of my hand and dragged me onto the safety of the sand away from the dangerous rocks, her scream at me expressed the fears and frustrations of her stressful life. She hit me across the legs with my small stick while we both cried and struggled, my hand tightly clutched in a firm grip with no possibility of escape until we had reached home. Authority had eventually caught up with me!

Mother's sister Eleni was very upset to see that I had been punished so severely. I was then washed and dressed in my best clothes and I'd soon stopped crying. My mother then hugged me and in tears, feeling guilty and now speaking very softly, tried to justify the punishment that she had inflicted upon me.

"Rather than me crying for him, let him cry for his disobedience and naughtiness!"

Mother believed in the old-fashioned principle that if you spare the rod, you spoil the child. The punishment had the desired effect. I never again strayed towards the dangerous rocks. Later, my sister used this prohibition as a means of controlling me. She often warned me,

"If you don't listen, I shall tell Mama that you went to the rocks again."

This was blackmail, but at the thought of being so severely punished again, I reluctantly obeyed my sister who was delighted that she could at last exert some kind of control over me. From then on, this threat was used by my sister to ensure that I didn't run out to the beach without her permission, and that at 2 pm, I would, without protest, go to my bed for a quiet rest or nap.

The rocks also became a kind of symbol between my mother and me so that as a child or even later in life when I became a man, if she felt that I was making an erroneous decision she would quietly utter,

"Fotaki, be careful, you are too close to the rocks. You will fall in and drown!"

Then she would step back and allow me to think about what I was doing. Of course, I understood her implied meaning.

1. Paniyiri – A village fare that takes place on the holy day of the patron saint of the village. The village people attend church on such a day when special prayers are dedicated to the patron saint of the village. This is followed with a celebration in the centre of the village. There is food and drink, music and song. Stalls are set up that sell cakes, sweets, nuts, toys. It is a family occasion when people gather together to enjoy each other's company.

2. Odysseus and the Cyclops – Odysseus is the hero of Homer's great epic, *The Odyssey*. It describes how Odysseus experienced many adventures and misfortunes on his way home to Ithaca after the sack of Troy. On one of his adventures, he confronts the dreadful Cyclops, Polyphemos the son of Posidon, "The next land we found were Kyklopes, giants, louts, without law to bless them." Book IX, lines 111-112. *The Odyssey*, Homer. Translated by Robert Fitzgerald. Everyman's Library.

3. Anthropophagi – Othello, the Moor of Venice, claimed that Desdemona loved him for the stories that he told her and one of these related to the anthropophagi: "And of cannibals that each other eat, the Anthropophagi." *Othello*. William Shakespeare, Act 1, Scene 3, lines 141-142. Heinemann. Homer also refers to the anthropophagi. They are the Laestregonians who attack Odysseus and his men with the purpose of devouring them. Antiphates, the King of the Laestregonians, "Came to drink their blood. He seized one man and tore him on the spot, making a meal of him…" *The Odyssey*, Homer. Book X, lines 129-130. Translated by Robert Fitzgerald. Every Man's Library.

4. The witch that turned men into beasts – Kirke is the witch that turns men into beasts. Odysseus's men suffer this cruel fate when they are enticed into her palace where they eat and drink and are bewitched and turned into pigs: "Scarce had they drank when she flew after them with her long stick and shut them in a pigsty – bodies, voices, heads and bristles, all swinish now though minds were still unchanged." Odysseus eventually rescues them from their terrible fate. *The Odyssey*, Homer. Book X, lines 262-265. Translated by Robert Fitzgerald. Every Man's Library.

Paniyiri

In the afternoon, we travelled to the paniyiri in Sotira. It was early August and we travelled the short journey from Varosi on a bus full of people heading for the celebration of the Feast Day of the Saviour.[1]

On our arrival, we found that the crowds had already gathered. There were many stalls selling sweets and cakes. Long sticks of delicious *soujouko*[2] were laid out on display. Trays of *galaktoboureka*[3] and *kalopragma*[4] tempted all those who walked by and looked upon them. There was cooling *mahalebi*[5] with a sprinkling of sugar and rose water. There was the smell of *souvlakia*[6] everywhere. People were sitting in the cafés, eating and drinking. Families in their best clothes were strolling through the festive streets. Girls in bright floral dresses walked hand in hand, boys with James Dean hair styles, in clean, crisp white shirts loitered in groups of two or three, trying to catch the attention of the girls who walked by and teasingly looked at them, children called out to each other and ran around playing their games. There was the sound of music and laughter as people greeted each other and stopped to speak in the village centre. This was the day of Hrisosotiros, the Golden Saviour, after whom the village was named. This was the day when men and women put their troubles behind them, at least for a few hours, for the purpose of worship and then for relaxation.

Here, my aunties and uncles with their children came to greet us. Mother was always delighted to be amongst her sisters. Each one had her own pronounced character: Eleni was the youngest and the loveliest. She was tall, slim and elegant with an air of intelligence about her. She darted around, arranging things, keeping an eye on the children and making sure that everything went smoothly. Christina was the most reserved. She spoke quietly and in moderate tones, avoiding gossip and loud people. She always stood close to her husband, my uncle Foti, as if she could not bear any physical distance between them. Filou always had a smile for every one and she was famous for her ability in the *tsatista*[8] songs. On the first occasion when I visited Cyprus as an adult and with my family, Auntie Filou invited us to her house for dinner. Not only was the food and wine delicious, but she also composed and sang many *tsatista* songs to welcome us to Cyprus. Auntie Martha was the most outspoken. She was very courageous and challenged anything that might be an injustice. Of all my aunties, she had a special warmth and kindness towards other people. She was always good company, full of interesting anecdotes and opinions. Mother and her sisters were known as the five sisters from Stylloi who had come to Sotira and claimed *Sotirkates*, men of Sotira, for husbands. Of all the women of the village, they were loved and respected most because they were honest, hardworking, generous and entertaining to be with, for when the sisters were together, they always created an atmosphere of enjoyment. They forgot the problems of life. They laughed, joked and they talked, sharing their news and plans with each other. The *Paniyiri of the Hrisosotiros* was the time when they walked out with their husbands and their children, with pride and dignity, to enjoy the society of the village and to interact with friends and relatives.

The festivities began in the afternoon as the sun was setting. It was a special day for the village, so people really wanted to celebrate and commune with each other. There was eating and drinking. Red wine produced at home and KEO 31 Cyprus cognac were consumed in great quantities, especially by the men who competed with each other in the singing of *tsatista* to the accompaniment of the violin, the lute and much hand clapping. Men danced the *Hasapiko*, hands outstretched, clicking fingers, stamping of feet, leaping and gyrating to the wailing music. The dance of the men was measured with masculine movements while the dance that followed, the *Kalamatiano*[9], was performed entirely by the women holding hands in a circle and moving delicately to the gentle feminine rhythms.

These dances were convenient. They fitted in well with the customs of village life because the sexes were kept at a distance to each other. It was inappropriate for the young men and women to dance, to talk or be seen together in a manner that could be misunderstood. But the young would always find a way to overcome the restrictions of their elders. They glanced at each other, smiled when passing by, indicating favour that one day could end in arranged marriage. Despite this, it was upheld without question that open interaction, even at a social community event, between unmarried young women and men who did not belong to the same family, was unacceptable and deeply frowned upon. Happily, however, the young man at church or at the market or at the paniyiri, whose gaze would be returned with acknowledgement by a young lady, while parents obliviously busied themselves with their day to day concerns, always had the option of speaking to his father to seek through a go between, usually a respected member of the community, the young women's hand in marriage. So, romance in the life of the village had very clear boundaries and according to the values of generations of village people, real romance could only flourish after a marriage and not before.

Eventually, the gratified villagers would begin to drift away from the village centre. They had eaten their fill of *souvlakia* and *kleftiko*. They had erased the after taste of pork and lamb with sweet meats. They had quenched their thirst with sweet red wine and Cyprus cognac. On that night we were going to stay at Auntie Filous' house. Feeling tired but satisfied with the prolonged festivities, we left the paniyiri and walked through the streets with the scent of jasmine hanging heavily in the air, under a glowing, white moon and a sky dotted with stars lighting our way. That night we went to sleep with the music of the Hasapiko and the Kalamatino still lulling and lingering in our heads while throughout the village, young men and women remained wakeful, thinking of that moment when the secret, surreptitious, sublime glance was exchanged between them and their chosen one.

1. The feast Day of the Saviour – This Christian festival celebrates the Transfiguration of Christ when He appears in radiant glory to his disciples. "There he was Transfigured before them. His face shone like the sun, and his clothes became as white as the light." Matthew 17:2. Holy Bible. New International Version.

2. Soujouko – It is made from boiled thick grape juice and it is produced in the shape of a sausage.

3. Galaktoboureko – A creamy custard pie with syrup with a covering of syrup.

4. Kalopragma – A semolina cake with syrup.

5. Mahalebi – Made with corn flour and immersed in rose water.

6. Hasabiko – A dance that in medieval Byzantium was performed by the butcher's guild. It is a slow and rhythmic dance originally performed with knives.

7. Souvlakia – Pieces of meat on a skewer, cooked on charcoal.

8. Tsatista – Improvised folk singing often accompanied by violin and lute.

9. Kalamatianos – An ancient dance that is characterised by forming a circle and holding hands. The leader of the dance carries a handkerchief that is held by the dancer following. There are many popular songs that are performed in the style of the Kalamatiano. These include 'Samiotissa' (Girl from Samos), 'Mantilli Kalamatiano' (Kerchief from Kalamata), 'Millo Mou Kokkino' (My red apple) and 'Orea pou einai i vimfi mas' (Beautiful is our bride) Greek Dances (Helliniki Hori) George H. Lykesas. Thessaloniki University Press, second edition, 1993.

Aunt Cornelia

In the morning of the following day, Mother took my sister and me to the village centre to buy us shoes because they were cheaper in the village then in Varosi. On the way to the shop, it chanced that we encountered my father's sister, Aunt Cornelia, carrying some bags of shopping, on her way home. She was a small woman with a cheerful face and piercing olive green eyes. She greeted us with a warm smile,

"*Kalimera sas.*"

She kissed my sister and me affectionately. She embraced Mother like a long-lost sister. Mother was rather surprised because Father's family had been against his marriage with Mother.

"You must come to the house, Andriana. My mother wants to see you and her grandchildren."

Something had obviously changed because their disapproval had now transformed into a fond embrace. She wouldn't take no for an answer and Mother soon relented. The house was only five minutes away and we were soon there.

"Come in, please come in," said my Aunt Cornelia, her sunburnt face beaming with an affectionate smile.

"Mother, where are you?" she called out towards the kitchen.

"Andrikou and the children are here."

Grandmother Margarita emerged from the kitchen, wiping the perspiration from her face with her apron. Like all the old ladies of the village who were widowed, she was dressed in the customary black. Her hair was tied back and covered with a *kouroukla*. She was stout and sturdy with strong hands that had been made hard by the constant labour on the land. Her intelligent eyes were deep set and sparkled with warmth.

"Kalosorisete, welcome my children. Why are you standing at the door like strangers? Come in and sit down."

We were there almost for the whole morning. They offered us sweets and drinks that refreshed us. Grandmother Margarita asked many questions about where we lived in Varosi, whether Mother had work and could support us. She also knew that Father was working for the British in the Suez Canal and asked whether he kept in contact with us. Mother didn't want to upset the old lady by telling her the truth that Father rarely sent us a letter or anything else.

"Yes, Mother, Loizos sends us letters and money. We receive something every month from him. Don't worry about us. I have a job and everything is fine."

Grandmother Margarita was not convinced.

"I am not so sure that everything is alright as you say. I know that Loizos can be very foolish at times. I don't know why he sold the materials I had purchased for him to build his house. Why did he do such a thing and now you and your children do not have a place to call your own? You are like birds without a nest."

Her eyes clouded and tears ran down her weather-worn cheeks at the thought of what her son had done and the implications for her daughter-in-law and her grandchildren. Mother took her hand and tried to reassure her that despite everything that had happened, things would turn out for the best.

"Mother, Loizos is sorry for what he has done. He is now going to be more responsible. We are both young and strong. We will work hard and build a new future. Don't think about what has happened. It is the past."

"May God, hear your words and help my son to become a better man for the sake of this children."

Grandmother Margarita spoke with feeling, conviction and honesty. She was pleased with Mother's brave little speech but she didn't believe it for a moment because she knew her son too well. She knew that one day, he could be mild, caring and loving and the next, he could be course, rough and selfish. She now looked at Mother with respect and admiration, clearly recognising that her son was very fortunate to be married to such a worthwhile person.

Their modern, brick-built house stood on the site where the old patriarchal dwelling had been for generations. The location was almost in the centre of the village, very close to the Church of the Hrisosotiros in which the villagers were baptised, where they married and eventually where prayers were said for their funerals. The houses closest in proximity to the church belonged to the oldest and most established members of the village whose importance was also measured in the ownership of the rich and fertile land, cultivated fields that produced an abundance of *Kolokasi[1]* and potatoes as well as water melons, and a variety of vegetables that were sold at the municipal market of Varosi and which made the farmers of the area amongst the wealthiest in Cyprus.

Later, after our visit, we laughed at how Aunt Cornelia had three or four children who each had one hand tied to the window frame by a kind of leash. She explained,

"There are passing cars and I don't want them to run out into the road, just in case."

Aunt Cornelia might have been anxious about the safety of her children but her fear of passing cars was misplaced and certainly an exaggeration because there were probably very few cars that went through the streets of Sotira at that time. Mother mused how the children had been tethered but that the only vehicle that had passed by the house was an old two-wheeled cart, drawn by an old mare. It moved so slowly along the road and it was unlikely that it would cause any serious accident.

Aunt Cornelia seemed happy enough when we visited her on that memorable occasion but she had gone through some problems which she would not have been able to sort out if it had not been for my father's actions. It might have been true that father had sometimes behaved in an irresponsible manner but he could also be very protective of the people whom he loved and cared for. Mother knew the story very well and often in an animated voice, as if the events had only happened yesterday, she would cast the plot in a manner that presented Father as a hero and his brother-in-law as a villain. The truth of the matter is that she may have expressed some bias in her version of events. We listened to her in silence while Mother thoroughly enjoyed the telling of the story:

"Old Kaiki was a very clever man in the village and he was also very fair. He had involved himself in civic matters and the villagers were so impressed by him that he became mayor, the *muchtari*[2] of the village. His sons were good, hardworking boys and, like their father, were very ambitious. One of them, Panayi, saw the opportunity to gain more land and property through marrying a woman who could provide him with such wealth and in the village," Mother continued.

"It was a well-known fact that Margarita, Cornelia's mother, at the death of her husband Pieris, had become the mistress of many plots of land around the village and beyond. The fields around Sotira were the most fertile in all the vicinity of the *Kokkinohoria*[3]. The earth, a rich copper colour, produced three harvests every year. The lush, deep green leaves of the Kolokasi plant, like miniature banana trees, resembled the plantations of the tropics rather than those of a dry Mediterranean island. Grandmother Margarita's numerous plots of land were located as far as Macronissos, Ayia Thekli and even Ayia Napa. Cornelia was not a great beauty, but she was wealthy and for Panayi this seemed the most important consideration. In due course, they were engaged and dear Cornelia soon fell pregnant. It is then that Panayi, began to show his true intentions. He wanted to get as much land as possible for marrying Cornelia and he was prepared to use blackmail."

At this point in the story, my mother would pause, smile and wait for a few seconds as if to create some kind of suspense in whoever was listening and even though I had heard this story a few times, the pause always worked well; I felt impatient for Mother to resume from where she had left off:

"He began to show a great reluctance concerning his proposed marriage to Cornelia and complained that her dowry, and by this he meant the amount of land that she would be given as her share on her wedding, was not enough. He threatened that he would not go through with the wedding unless this dowry was substantially increased. You can imagine how the poor, perplexed and pregnant Cornelia felt. She was carrying a child; her growing womb was already quite prominent and very noticeable, yet her fiancé was threatening to abandon her unless more land was surrendered. He had no shame and his greed prevented him from seeing the distress that he was causing to his pregnant fiancée and her mother. They didn't know what to do, they were at their wits end. And you must remember," Mother added in a very serious, matter of fact tone, "unmarried mothers in Cyprus at that time were looked down upon as a disgrace and in that village to have a child and no husband was a huge dishonour for the family. There would be no sympathy, no understanding, no kindness from anyone. As usual in Cyprus, at that time and very unfairly, the man had his pleasure, and if he did not behave honourably, the woman was abandoned with the child and was looked upon as a person of ill repute. Well, this is when Loizos, my husband, took things into his own hands. When he heard what was happening from his mother, he obtained a pistol from God knows where and he let it be known that he was going to deal with Panayi if he dared to break his promise to marry his sister."

Mother paused and smiled at the memory of her young husband, who on that occasion was decisive, determined and brave enough to take extreme action for the honour of his sister and the family. The Kaiki brothers were numerous and could have responded in a violent manner. They were no easy pushover.

Mother continued, "Loizos took up position on a rooftop near Panayi's home, apparently with serious intent. Very soon after, Panayi withdrew his threat to abandon his fiancée and the wedding went ahead as planned. But this was not the end of the story. From the moment that my husband had interfered in this matter, Panayi developed an utter hatred for him. He and his brothers refused to allow him to attend the wedding of his sister and there was a probability that from that time onwards, he tried very hard to claim even my husband's share of the inheritance."

My mother finished the telling of this story with an expression of anger and defiance on her face because she felt that we had been cheated by Panayi of what rightfully belonged to my father. She felt outrage, unfairness and injustice. Years after, when as a retired pensioner she returned to Sotira, she made her feelings clear that not only the plots of land that were my father's share of the inheritance had somehow ended up belonging to Panayi, but even the land upon which the house that Panayi inherited through marriage was a part of my father's share and had been stolen from him. She openly claimed that her children had been robbed and deprived of their inheritance. Mother's claims were taken so seriously that Panayi's sons began to threaten this elderly woman, a widow and alone, who had returned to her husband's village after many years of living in a foreign land. Nothing came from the claims that Mother had made simply because she didn't have any documents to prove ownership. When the matter was investigated at the local land registry, Mother's feeling was that while the Kaiki family had been influential in the local government and the administration of village affairs, the documents and deeds showing my father's entitlement had been altered in favour of his sister and her husband Panayi. Of course, it may be that our grandmother Margarita and Aunt Cornelia had a hand in this because once the wedding had taken place and Panayi proved himself to be a good husband to Cornelia, they might have felt that it was only sensible to protect as much as possible of the family wealth and to prevent Father from getting his hands onto it. Aunt Cornelia and Grandmother Margarita might have felt that had he done so, it may have all been squandered in the gambling houses or the cabarets of Nicosia. On the other hand, it isn't absolutely certain that Father would have behaved in such a way.

Despite the support he had given his sister during the crisis of her engagement, Father's family were convinced, rightly or wrongly, that he had made mistakes and that he would continue to so; there would be no redemption or miraculous change in his wayward character. They were uncomfortable with his attitude and they saw very clearly that Mother was a very decent and hardworking woman. They saw that she loved her children and cared for her husband, but he, on the other hand, was not to be trusted with property or money.

Many years after, I was to return to the family house in Sotira. I was welcomed by its sole occupant, Panayi, who was now an old man and the widowed husband of my Aunt Cornelia. Even as an eighty-year-old, he seemed sharp, alert and focused. He was very aware of what was going on around him. When we met, I called him uncle and tried to show my respect towards him to allay any fears that he may have had that I had returned like my mother, to start making claims on the house in which he had lived for over fifty years. Even so, though he smiled graciously, he could not hide, I felt, his suspicion that I had returned to cause him some problems. He smiled and spoke politely but he glanced at me uneasily and had a strained expression on his face. Because I knew the details of the story, I understood why Panayi may have been suspicious about my visit to Sotira.

Panayi's neighbour had been my father's brother, Uncle George, who had been born and had always remained in the same house and had only left the village for very brief periods to journey to the nearby towns on some essential business or other. Uncle George was a stout, bald man with a rim of grey hair that stretched like a ribbon around the base of his head to just above his ears. His large, khaki brown eyes and bald head gave him the appearance of an ancient Greek philosopher. His crisp and witty speech added to the impression that he was an intelligent man. During my visit, I ventured to ask my uncle his views about my mother's claims. Uncle George had explained that the plot of land, upon which the house that Aunt Cornelia occupied, was my father's but he had sold it to her and Panayi.

"Fotaki," my uncle addressed me in a formal manner befitting the serious subject of land ownership.

"Your father was never one to hold on to money for very long. He did not want the difficult life of a farmer. From the very beginning, he did not want to stay here in this village. He sold the plot to our sister and I know this for certain because I was present at the discussion of this matter."

Uncle George was very direct and to the point regarding what had taken place. Mother claimed that he was not to be trusted and that he was in league with Panayi to cheat his own brother. She claimed that the plot for Father's house belonged to him by right of inheritance but the Kaiki family had had the documents falsified in favour of Cornelia and thus under the control of Panayi, her husband. The truth of the matter is unclear, and I have often asked the question to my sister that if Father had not sold the plot for his house, why had he never said that we had a right to it. He remained very quiet on the subject. To further complicate matters, after some years when we had settled in England, we were visited by Father's brother-in-law, the very same Panayi who Father had threatened with a pistol regarding the fulfilment of his promise to marry Father's sister. This was now forgotten. He visited our house as if he was a long-lost friend. He was on a visit to three of his brothers who lived in Nottingham and he said that he could not come all the way to England and not also pay a goodwill visit to his own beloved brother-in-law. Mother sensed that of all the possible reasons why Panayi would go to so much trouble to come to see us, goodwill was the least likely. Mother was highly suspicious of what transpired between Father and Panayi. We have often puzzled over the possibility that some transaction was carried out regarding Father's property in Cyprus. In addition to the house plot that Uncle George said that Father had sold to his sister, there were many acres of land that should have belonged to Father. However, Father was always a closed book on this matter and never spoke to us about it. Therefore, when Mother made claims to Father's inheritance in Sotira, though she was brave, courageous and determined to gain for her children what she felt was their inheritance, she was unable to act with any certainty. In fact, as far as the legality of the claim was concerned, she didn't have a leg to stand on!

Near to the house that should have been my father's was the old cemetery inside the compound of the church where generations of our family had been laid to rest. The village of Sotira was where our ancestors were born, where they grew, worked, married, had children and at the end of their lives, had been laid to rest. This little corner of the world was where we belonged; it was where we had deep, strong roots up to that point in time. It seems, however, that when Father had lost his inheritance and particularly the plot of land upon which his matrimonial home was intended to be built, he also thoughtlessly and selfishly tore out the roots that we, his family, could have had with the place where our forefathers had lived for generations. What he did then, without a doubt, was the first step towards us becoming refugees. First was the move from Sotira, where Father had been a member of an established family, to Stylloi, where we lived in a house that was rented. There was no work available in this village and eventually it was decided to move to Varosi, and from there, again for the same reasons, we embarked for England. We became a family uprooted from its native soil, people who no longer had a precise geographical location, exiles and outcasts, who like the wandering Jews of yesteryear, would never again belong to a locality in the same sense as our grandparents had belonged to their communities. We became a part of the great movement of people who, because of war or famine or lack of hope, are forced to move. Throughout history, there have been these endless waves of people in search of safety and shelter; searching for hope, searching for the promised land.

It was much later, in a different environment, that I gradually began to have a sense that when plants are torn from their native soil, some, the very old or the very established, suffer and die because they cannot again develop new roots in an alien soil. But there are also seedlings or young plants that acclimatise, take root in the new earth, nourish on its richness, establish themselves, grow, blossom and eventually bear fruit. Such would be our experience as we looked beyond the shores of our

Mediterranean homeland, towards the northern climes, towards other seas, different skies, towards England.

1. Kolokasi – Colocasia Escalunta. In English it is called Taro and it originates from southeast Asia. It is a type of potato that is widely cultivated in Sotira and the surrounding villages.
2. Muchtari – A Turkish word for demarchos or mayor.
3. Kokkinohoria – The 'red villages' given this name because of the colour of their soil. The closest main town is now Larnaca. Prior to the Turkish invasion of 1974, the main town had been Varosi. The villages are Paralimni, Protaras, Derynia, Agia Napa, Frenaros, Sotira, Leopetri, Avgorou and Xylofagou.

A Bloody History

The Second World War had ended in 1945 and a new, more prosperous Europe was beginning to emerge from the dust and devastation of war. Even though there was also peace in Cyprus, the people suffered dire economic conditions and to cap it all, Cyprus continued to be in the possession of another country. Europe had been liberated but the Cypriots were still in bondage, they had masters who ruled and looked down upon them. Many felt the injustice of this condition. The people were hungry, down trodden, exploited and hardly better than slaves. How long could such circumstances be tolerated?

At the beginning of the 1950s, Cyprus remained a British Crown Colony. There had been attempts in the past, rightly or wrongly, to unite the island with Greece, but these attempts were unsuccessful and only resulted in the bloody suppression of the people.

It was a time when, apart from the Soviet Bloc, nationalism was the predominant political ideology in most countries in the world. In Cyprus, all moderate and reasonable arguments relating to the need for a Cypriot identity were brushed aside with contempt. This complicated matters for the political developments on the island. Anyone who spoke of the common heritage of Greek and Turkish Cypriots was branded a traitor by their own community and was in danger of being killed by the nationalist extremists who were daring, dangerous and were determined to derail any attempts to promote unity between the two main Cypriot communities. They regarded the advocates of bi-communalism to be anathema to their cause. The two extreme nationalist organisations that came into being were EOKA[1], whose aim was to achieve union with Greece by making both the British and the Turkish Cypriots concede to this demand. Turkish Cypriot nationalists, the TMT[2] had no intention of conceding anything to the Greek Cypriots and set about implementing their own plan which was to partition the island and to set up their own political entity.

The opposing dynamics of the two communities had their origins in the bloody history of the island and unfortunately as Cyprus emerged into the 20th century, it seemed unable to shake off the effects of its painful past. Very sadly, the true and courageous Cypriot patriots, people like

Costas Mishaolis and Dervis Ali Kavazoglu[3], who fought for bi-communalism and a Cypriot identity, were savagely murdered. The voices of the moderate and reasonable people who wanted a peaceful development to independence and a fair and democratic sharing of power were silenced. There was no opportunity given for the point of view to be proclaimed and for the people to understand and grasp the concept that Cyprus belonged to the ethnic communities of Cyprus who could, in unity, forge a common destiny. Instead of unity, mistrust and division, hostility and alienation, hatred and fear were nurtured by the fanatics who delivered their message that Greeks and Turks could never live together. The fanatics used history as a propaganda tool to manipulate the minds of the people and to point to how unjustly they had been treated and how it was impossible to find reconciliation. The participation of the Greek Cypriots in the Greek War of Independence and its bloody suppression by the Ottoman authorities is an example of how history was used to inflame political passions and hatred to the point where perfectly reasonable people were prepared to murder their neighbours.

The extreme mistrust between the two communities during the modern era may be traced back to how the Greek Cypriots had attempted to join the Greeks in their fight for independence from the Ottoman Empire and the bloody reaction of the authorities to snuff out any challenge to their power. This historical event was used by the Greek Cypriot nationalists to show how the Ottomans had engaged in bloody suppression of the Greeks who were fighting for their freedom. This is true but to use historical events that happened in the past as a way of inciting hatred in the present is unethical from the point of view that history should teach us not to make the same mistakes again. The Turkish Cypriot nationalists used the same event to illustrate how the Greek Cypriots could not be trusted because their only aim was to drive the Turkish Cypriots out of Cyprus.

Let us consider the following:

When the Greek War of Independence broke out in 1821, to pre-empt any difficulties with the populace of Cyprus, the Sultan authorised the execution of the leading members of Cypriot society. On the 9th of July of that tumultuous year, 486 prominent Christians including the Ethnarch, Archbishop Kyprianos, having been severely and cruelly tortured by the Ottoman authorities, were marched in the scorching midday sun, wounded, bleeding and bound in chains. They were marched to Sarai Square of Nicosia. The citizens of the capital had a sleepless and fearful night before the dawn of the day of the execution of their leaders. Families sat huddled together through the long night in fear of attack or even of massacre from the heavily armed Moslems who stopped at nothing in order to retain their control of the island.

Later that day, under the gaze of the terrified citizens of the capital, the Archbishop and the leaders of the church were offered their lives in return for denouncing the Christian faith and becoming followers of Islam. The proud and triumphant Kuchuk Pasha, the leader of the Turks, called out so that all could hear his offer:

"Those of you who will turn away from the cross and worship Allah the Almighty and Merciful, kiss the Koran, bow to Mohammed the Prophet and live as Moslems amongst us, will be spared from execution!"

The Bishops of the church with their Archbishop knelt together for the last time and prayed to Christ for the forgiveness of their sins and for the redemption of their souls. After their prayers, they walked in quiet dignity to their executions. Some prisoners were decapitated while others and amongst these the Ethnarch were hanged on the branch of a mulberry tree. Not one of them had renounced his faith for the sake of his life. The blood from those who were beheaded flowed in streams and gathered in pools. One by one, while they called out to the *Panayia* or to Christ, their heads were cut off with a heavy sword, the *palla;* their heads were stacked into a pile that formed a pyramid. Heavily armed gangs of irregular Moslem militia continued to mercilessly beat those still awaiting execution. They screamed at the prisoners and at the stunned on-lookers,

"Where is your Christos to save you? Where is your *Panayia* now? Embrace Almighty and Merciful Allah so that your worthless lives can be spared!"

The prisoners were prepared to die but they were not prepared to betray Christ or the *Panayia*. As if to inflict further pain on those who had been tortured and killed, the headless bodies on the floor and hanging bodies from the tree were left in the square for days before their families were allowed to retrieve them for burial.

The Christian population had good reason to fear. The execution of their leaders could have been a preamble to a general massacre, a method which had been previously used to control the subjects of the sultan. Thus, the people remained subdued and quiet in the face of the horrors and threats that they were facing. They needed, much against their true feelings which burnt for liberty, to reassure the Ottoman authorities that they were nothing more than the loyal subjects of the sultan. Submissiveness was the only realistic response to an overwhelming and tyrannical power that could unleash unopposed, unlimited, unprovoked terror on the defenceless people.

Gradually, the fear of rebellion died down and the blood lust of the masters was allayed. Thousands had been massacred while others fled west to the safety of the Ionian Islands. Eventually, new church leaders were selected who swore loyalty to the sultan and life began to return to

63

normal. The people resumed their everyday preoccupations as shop keepers, artisans, as farmers tilling the soil, sowing the seed and harvesting the produce of the earth and despite the hardships of life, they worshiped steadfastly in their Orthodox Christian faith, giving thanks to God for all that they received. But the nightmare of the event was never forgotten.[3]

This story presents the events of 1821. The Greek Cypriots can argue that the story contains facts about the events relating to executions and massacres of Greek Cypriots at that time. At the same time, the Turkish Cypriots could point out that in the real political world, where there had been rebellions against the authority of the rulers, the response was always to suppress such rebellions for the sake of maintaining power. This is politics, history and human nature; this is how people have behaved in the past and continue to do so today. We can understand both reactions to unfortunate historical events, but to take this history, to redesign it as a tool for creating hate, as has been done by the Greek Cypriot and Turkish Cypriot nationalists, is unethical, immoral and a crime against the people who are the victims of history used as propaganda, propaganda which has led to the false premise that the two communities of Cyprus cannot live together, and their fate is to always distrust and hate each other.

The oppression and massacre of the defenceless Greek Cypriots in 1821 had without a doubt led to their reluctance to think of Turkish Cypriots as fellow Cypriots. The crumbling of the British Empire after the Second World War should have led to the unity of the two communities in a struggle for independence. Fighting together for an independent, common homeland could have wiped the slate clean from past enmity between the two sides. Instead, the seeds of mistrust and fear that had been sown by the massacres of 1821 led the Greek Cypriots to seek greater security in a union with Greece and for the Turkish Cypriots to oppose such an outcome by joining forces with the British to fight against Greek Cypriot aspirations while pursuing their own policy to partition Cyprus.

It is clear that the bloodshed of 1821 has led to further bloodshed in the 20th century because there was no one to present an alternative. The lesson to be learnt by the two Cypriot communities, even at this late stage, is that with a little more compassion and understanding, with more enlightened political attitudes, much could have been done to heal the wounds from the past. Passed enmity doesn't have to go on forever. There are examples where people have made the choice that despite a bloody past, cooperation and friendship can be achieved. The European Union is made up of countries that not so long ago were slaughtering each other. We remember the names of such battles as Verdun and the Somme which took place during World War 1 and in which hundreds of thousands of young men were sent to certain death. A whole generation of young men, in the flower of youth, were cut down in the bloodiest battles the world has ever experienced. It was tribalism at its worst. Yet the hate, the blood lust and the desire to destroy each other has been replaced by unity, cooperation, partnership and respect. This can be seen in the partnership and work of Francois Mitterrand, the French President (1981–1995) and Helmut Kohl, the German Chancellor (1982–1998), who were the key promoters of the Maastricht Treaty (1992) that advanced European integration and the reunification of Germany (1990). The page of the bloody history of the 20th century had been turned. The new order and reality was now one of reconciliation. The weapons of war were cast asunder and in unity, the former enemies achieved the greatest peace in Europe since the days of *PAX ROMANA*[4]. It can also happen in Cyprus. Our divisions are not so great that they cannot be overcome!

~

Some years after the execution of the Ethnarch Archbishop Kyprianos[5], news arrived and spread like wild fire across the island: Greece had gained its liberty, Greece had become a state[6]. This sudden and dramatic news rekindled the hope that one day Cyprus could also gain its freedom but, for the moment, Cyprus remained under the oppressive Ottoman rule until the coming of the British, which would not be for another fifty years. Ironically, during the First World War, the British were to offer Cyprus to Greece in return for Greek support in the Balkans. The Greeks declined but later, nevertheless, entered the war on the side of the British. They had, however, lost the opportunity of gaining Cyprus and the offer was not to be repeated. There was a failure in the political understanding of the Greek state. Greece had failed to comprehend that it was never in a position to gain what it wanted or to become what it aspired to be. It had turned down the only time when it was actually possible to gain the island perhaps under some kind of mistaken illusion that this could be achieved at some later date.

The reality for Greece is that it is a small country with limited military and economic means and in most circumstances, would not be able to compete with the more powerful predatory powers around her borders. This failure to comprehend harsh realities led to the catastrophe in Asia Minor during 1919–1923, when thousands of Greeks lost their lives and more than two million Greeks of Asia Minor were forced to abandon their homes in the new Turkish Republic and to resettle in Greece.

As if such a national catastrophe was not enough, the Greek state, against all logic, attempted to gamble with the fate of Cyprus without taking into consideration that the other players in the game of political and strategic poker held much more powerful hands and that the future of Cyprus would be put into jeopardy. In 1974, Greece predictably lost the game and Cyprus paid the heavy price by having one third of its territory occupied and 200,000 of its people made refugees in their own home land. Unfortunately, there is no end as yet to the saga of the Cyprus tragedy and the people of the island continue to struggle for a just settlement that seems both remote and unlikely.

~

As an adult, I now have a different understanding of the recent history of Cyprus and of the sad events that culminated in atrocities, bloodshed, war and division. The people of Cyprus had been exploited and misguided. The Cypriots of both communities did not understand that they had more in common with each other than with their respective 'motherlands'. They fell victim to the false Gods of nationalism. The small, quiet voice of reason that declared Cyprus to be the common motherland of Cypriots and to whom loyalty should be shown through the advancement of a common destiny was drowned in blood. I see this now, but it was not always so apparent. The truth fell victim to the nationalist propagandists from both sides who claimed that the other side were incarnate devils who had to be defeated at any cost. In time, most Cypriots including myself, have understood that the propaganda of the ultra-nationalists who supported hate and division were nothing more than lies that most of us once found to be believable. How could we have been so gullible? How could we have allowed matters to get so out of hand? Unhappily, for me the questions remain:

Will the land be whole again?

Will the Greek and Turkish Cypriots ever be able to break free from the negative influence of their so-called 'motherlands' and declare their true identity which is to be Cypriot without the qualifying adjective?

Will the Cypriots ever be able to forge a common identity?

Will we ever have politicians like Francois Mitterrand and Helmut Kohl who will turn the page of division and hate and achieve unity and peace?

Indeed, there are more questions than answers.

1. E.O.K.A. – Ethniki Organosis Kiprion Agoniston (National organisation of Cypriot fighters). This was a military organisation that fought the British Army during 1956–1959. It was led by Colonel George Grivas. Its aim was to unite Cyprus with Greece.

This objective was entitled 'Enosis' which simply means 'union'. The political struggle for Enosis was headed by Archbishop Makarios who gave his support and encouragement to Colonel Grivas and E.O.K.A. It must also be said that at that time, the vast majority of Greek Cypriots who represented 82% of the islands entire population, supported the movement for Enosis. In my opinion, Enosis was never a viable objective. It was doomed to failure because neither Britain nor Turkey were prepared to let it happen. The failure of the Greeks and Greek Cypriots to understand their political and military limitations led to the Turkish invasion and tragic events of 1974.

2. T.M.T. (Turk Mukavemet Testilati) – The T.M.T. was founded in 1957 with the aim of fighting E.O.K.A. and in response to the demands of the Greek Cypriots. The policy of T.M.T. was to divide the island into Greek Cypriot and Turkish Cypriot sectors so that the interests and identity of the Turkish Cypriot population, who felt that the Greek Cypriots who outnumbered them on a ratio of 4 to 1, could be protected. This policy was called 'Taksim' which when translated into English means partition. Though they represented the two opposing sides, there was much in common between E.O.K.A. and T.M.T. Both organisations were extreme nationalistic; they were loyal to the interests and policies of the so-called motherlands, Greece or Turkey. They tried to suppress and silence with violence, terror or murder, any attempt to express the idea of an independent Cyprus as the common motherland of the Greek Cypriots and the Turkish Cypriots. Costas Misiaoulis who was Greek Cypriot and Dervis Kavazoglu who was Turkish Cypriot, were two journalists who belonged to AKEL and who were determined to work towards overcoming the divisions caused by nationalism and to unite the two communities through a vision of a common future. On the 11th of April 1965, they were both murdered by the agents of the TNT. Further, the Turkish Cypriot journalist, Sener Levent, points to the ruthless methods employed by the T.M.T. when in an interview with a senior commander of that organisation it is revealed that the famous bath-tub photo showing the dead mother and her children was set up by the T.M.T. It is also claimed that the position of the bodies was altered to make the photographs more effective for the purpose of arousing hatred towards the Greek Cypriots and inciting further inter-communal violence. Africa newspaper, 4th January, 2015 and Politis newspaper, 7th January, 2015. Equally, E.O.K.A. also targeted its own people usually on the pretext that they were

traitors or for belonging to A.K.E.L. the communist party of Cyprus, which was the only political party whose membership was from both the Greek Cypriot and Turkish Cypriot communities.

3. The Swedish traveller and writer, Jacob Bergren, describes the execution of Archbishop Kyprianos and the bloody events that follow. The events he describes are based on eye witness accounts shortly after they had occurred. 'Archbishop Kyprianos and the 9th July, 1821'. Hellenic Antidote.

4. PAX ROMANA, Roman Peace was a period of relative peace and stability across the Roman Empire which lasted for over two hundred years beginning with the reign of Augustus in 27 BCE. Ancient History Encyclopaedia. Pax Romana. Donald L. Wassoon.

5. Archbishop Kyprianos. He was the Archbishop of Cyprus until his execution in 1821. He is remembered for the promotion of education in Cyprus and for the establishment of the Pan Cyprian Gymnasium. This became the oldest secondary school in Cyprus and was originally called the Hellenic School. The Archbishop is also remembered for his association with the Filiki Eteria, an organisation that was dedicated to the overthrow of Ottoman power over Greek Christians and the establishment of the modern Greek State. When the rebellion of the Greeks began in 1821 the suspicion of Cypriot support for this cause triggered Ottoman reprisals. Though Archbishop Kyprianos was offered a safe passage into exile, he chose to remain with his flock knowing that his execution was a certainty. Orthodox Wiki "Historical Album of the Greek War of Independence 1821." George Tsoulios, Tassos Hadjis. Mellissa, Athens.

6. Independence of Greece, Treaty of Constantinople, 1832.

Part 2: The Journey

Father

In1956, my father decided, like many other Cypriots, to immigrate to England in the hope of building a better future. The economy of Cyprus during the 1950s remained stagnant and backward. There were few opportunities for ordinary people to improve their standard of living. The majority of the population lived in poverty without any real hope of a better future. In contrast to the conditions in Cyprus, the United Kingdom at this time was experiencing an economic boom. The country was rebuilding and re-modernising. Industry was working at full capacity and it needed a bigger labour force. People came from all parts of the empire to feed the demands of industry, the health service, the transport system. They came from India, the Caribbean, from Africa and they also came from the towns and villages of Cyprus.

Mother did not link the poverty that we suffered with any historical phenomenon. As far as she was concerned, the present was enough to think about. She blamed Father for our predicament because she knew that had he built a house in Sotira, life would still not have been entirely without problems, but we would have managed. We would have had our own house; Father was a craftsman, a shoemaker, so he could have had some kind of income from that. He stood to inherit some plots of land that he could have cultivated, growing vegetables and potatoes for the market in Varosi. Other families were able to do this so why could not we? When Mother thought about what could have been, she would bitterly admonish him. Father remained unrepentant.

"I am not going to labour in the fields to be scorched by the sun just to make a few *rials*. And I didn't want to stay in that dusty village with its uncouth people. I want to go to England. At least there I can find employment and live like a man. It will be better for all of us, believe me."

"If you don't have enough sense in your head to build a life in your own country, how will you do it in a foreign land?" Mother answered, unconvinced by his shallow argument.

"Many men are going to England!" my father shouted back. "They are not afraid, their wives are happy and give them encouragement. I will go first, find a job, a place to live and then you and the children can join me.

What's wrong with that? But all you can do is admonish me. We need to do this for our children."

At times like these, if you were an outsider and knew nothing of our family history, it would sound as if Father was the most reasonable and congenial person in the whole of Cyprus and that Mother was a difficult person who was hard to please. Admittedly, Father had his charming and persuasive side that he sometimes used to get what he wanted, and this was one of those occasions.

Mother looked at him, feeling uncomfortable and uncertain of his proposal. To leave Cyprus, to leave her parents and her sisters, to leave her familiar world to go to England, where she could not even speak the language and with a husband who was not totally reliable seemed to be a gamble in which she would be a certain loser. In the end it was Father's charm, persuasion and endless coercion that carried the day!

~

My father came to England with a family who had lived in a baranga next to ours in Varosi: Kalisteni, her husband Prokopis and her children Thomas, George, Costakis and Anna. They came together to an address and to jobs that had already been arranged for them. Mother had spent what little money she had to buy Father a new suit, some shirts, and a tie. Carrying a suitcase in one hand and a bag containing his shoe maker tools in the other, he arrived at Victoria Station. It was on the evening of 27th January, 1956.

In later years, he often told the story of an incident that occurred just after getting off the train. He described the occurrence with some amusement, probably at the thought of his own naivety. At the time, he took it to be a sign of the good fortune that he would find in this new land of hope:

"I'd just got off the train. It was freezing cold and I didn't have an overcoat. There were hundreds, thousands of people all around. This was London, the greatest city in the world and I'd never seen so many people in one place before. My long journey was over, and I was ready for my new life in this great city."

Every time he told this story, even when he was an old man, the beginning always sounded animated and exciting as if he was experiencing the moment of his arrival in England again.

"As I made my way out of the station, I looked down and there, in front of me, at my very feet, I saw a wallet that had been dropped by some unlucky person. I felt too proud to pick it up. I smiled, thinking that in this land people were not so desperate and that I would have better fortune just around the corner."

It wasn't long before he realised that the years ahead would be difficult, and that progress could only be achieved with sacrifices, even in England.

His passport stated his name: Loizos Pieris Loizou. His date of birth was the 5th of November, 1923 and that he was a citizen of the United Kingdom and Colonies. At the time of arrival, he was thirty-three years old. The photograph in his passport showed a handsome and well-dressed man in the prime of life, a man who might engage with the struggle against poverty and who might succeed.

When my father came to England in search of a better future, he was following the small number, a trickle of Cypriots who had immigrated to England even before the Second World War. Both Greek and Turkish Cypriots in larger numbers were now seriously thinking of leaving Cyprus. Like all refugees, they shared the same dream. They wanted to find a place of safety, security, to work, to build some kind of prosperous and worthwhile life. And so, my father followed in the footsteps of the refugees; the hundreds of thousands, the millions who have always existed in our world, crossing oceans and continents like migratory birds in search of new nests.

~

The tide of Cypriots coming to England coincided with political problems and bloodshed on the island. In fact, economic stagnation, unemployment, poverty and the outbreak of political violence had all greatly contributed to the decision of thousands of Cypriots from all backgrounds to leave their motherland and to seek a home elsewhere. People wanted to feel safe and they also felt that they deserved something better than constant economic hardship.

The political crisis had come again to the boiling point in1955. The aspiration for union with Greece had been supported even by the British during the First World War but had been rejected by Greece. It was, therefore, reasonable to assume that given the right circumstances, the dream of Enosis could somehow be achieved.

The young people of Cyprus, both Greek Cypriot and Turkish Cypriots had answered the call to arms to fight alongside Britain and its allies against Nazism and Fascism in Europe. Thirty thousand Cypriots fought as members of the British Army. They fought and some Greek Cypriots died in the belief that Cyprus would, in due course, be united with Greece. However, it must be said that this could not have been the aspiration of their fellow Turkish Cypriot comrades in arms who also made equal sacrifices against fascism and who obviously would not have seen eye to eye regarding the aspiration to join Greece. Was this so difficult to understand and to take into consideration? Shouldn't there have been some thought given to the response to such a move by other interested parties and more importantly, how they would have responded?

Despite these obvious questions, in 1940, Greece was the only country in Europe which was actively engaged in the war on the side of Britain and after the war, the Greek Cypriots felt that the union with Greece should be granted. The simple questions regarding the Turkish Cypriots were not considered with any seriousness. The church behaved as if these concerns did not exist and continued to pursue the goal of union with Greece. In 1950, a plebiscite engineered by the young and energetic Ethnarch, Archbishop Makarios. 96% voted in favour of union with Greece. This was not a new political sentiment. The Cypriots had tried to align themselves with the 1821 War of Greek independence, but they were geographically too far from the Aegean to be supported and had been brutally crushed by the Ottomans. In 1931, there were ferocious riots in support of Enosis. The burning down of Government House had led the British to suspend the representative council of the Cypriots. The British Government now seemed determined that Enosis should not be achieved.

The Greek Cypriots continued to behave as if the Turkish Cypriots did not have an opinion on the subject of Enosis or if they did, that it could be ignored. The Turkish Cypriots were understandably totally against such a fate and Turkey would not have needed much encouragement to get involved in the matter. Therefore, it should have been apparent to the Greek Cypriots that though union with Greece might have been their nationalistic dream, right or wrong, it was a dream too difficult to achieve even though they made up eighty percent of the population because Turkey was powerful enough to prevent its realisation. The geographical distance from Greece and the proximity to the Turkish mainland added to the immense difficulties of achieving Enosis and these are the same reasons why Cyprus was defenceless and did not play any significant role in the Greek War of Independence. Apart from this, there is the question of the fairness. Was it fair that the Greek Cypriots should have aspired to Enosis when the Turkish Cypriots were very much opposed? Should their fears not have been taken into consideration? Or was it fair when the Greek War of Independence was declared, that the Turkish Cypriots with the Ottomans should have carried out a massacre of the Greek Cypriots as a pre-emptive action to prevent the outbreak of rebellion on the island in sympathy with the rebellion in Greece? It seems that both communities have a story to tell about the injustice that they have suffered and both sides speak the truth.

To make matters worse, when the British Government was faced with the Greek Cypriot rebellion, in order to contain the situation, it clumsily resorted to the common tactics of the colonial master: divide and rule. It stoked the fires of Turkish Cypriot fears that they would be wiped out or pushed into the sea by their Greek Cypriot neighbours. To deliberately exasperate an already tense situation, the British Government recruited hundreds of Turkish Cypriots into the colonial police force for the purpose of controlling the rebellious Greek Cypriots. The final and most outrageous action that the British Government inflicted on Cyprus was to awaken the sleeping giant Turkey, who up to that moment, had had very little to say about Cyprus and to encourage it to become involved with the problems of the island.

From that time onwards, the eventual invasion by Turkey and the division of Cyprus became only a matter of time. It would have been far better for all concerned if the two communities had somehow been convinced of the advantages of being united and independent. This surely should have been the correct response from the ruling power in Cyprus. It didn't happen because it was not in its interest.

A divided Cyprus, with Greek Cypriots and Turkish Cypriots locked perpetually in inter-communal conflict would make it easy for the British Government to control the island for its own strategic interests. The British Sovereign Bases and the electronic listening stations in the Troodos Mountains were more important for the British Government than the welfare of the people of Cyprus. More should have been done to keep them united. In particular, a common education policy that promoted the sense of unity amongst the communities of Cyprus during the years of British Rule could have resulted in the Cypriots recognising themselves as Cypriot first and foremost rather than as Cypriot with a descriptive adjective attached. If the French, Italian and German citizens of Switzerland are happy to be Swiss, why cannot the Greek Cypriots and Turkish Cypriots be happy to embrace being Cypriots? Alas, it hasn't happened so far; the division of the people of Cyprus has occurred and continuous to this day. Despite the difficulties, there are those who continue to work for reconciliation; their voices have not been silenced as they continue to work for a common motherland.[1] Who knows if these seeds of trust and unity will one day grow into a united, happy and prosperous homeland?

1. Koray Bosodogrultmaci and Cinel Senem Husseyin were prosecuted by the authorities in the north because they flew the flag of the Republic of Cyprus outside of their home and their place of work. They insisted that they had done nothing wrong because they were Cypriot citizens flying the Cypriot flag in Cyprus. Cyprus Mail, 14th May 2015 also Phileleftheros, May 2015, Antigoni Solomonidou Drousioti. We can see how this couple, Koray and Sinel have endangered their lives in the face of fanatic nationalists for the sake of promoting the idea of a united Cyprus for all Cypriots. Another great fighter for Cyprus unity is Stelios Hajioannou who has founded the Stelios Philanthropic Foundation that encourages and rewards joint business enterprises between Greek speaking and Turkish speaking Cypriots. There are also the countless men and women of Cyprus from both communities who, when given the opportunity, will take to the streets and call for a fair resolution to the Cyprus problem and for a united motherland for all Cypriots. It is to be noted that the pro-unity movement were very vociferous in support of the negotiations for unity that culminated on the 2017 Cyprus congress in Crans-Montana, Switzerland. Unfortunately, much to the disappointment of the pro-unity movement, the talks were a failure and so the saga of the Cyprus problem continuous.

Teddy Boys

Father's arrival in London was just after the EOKA campaign had begun in Cyprus on 1st April, 1955. Not long after when EOKA had started to target British soldiers or personnel, the Cypriots in London, not surprisingly, had suddenly become very unpopular with the local people. There were racist attacks on individuals. Cypriots were offensively called 'bubbles'. They became the focus of attention of the 'teddy boy' thugs who used any excuse to intimidate, insult or physically attack innocent immigrants including the Cypriots who had left Cyprus to avoid the uncertainties of their strife-torn island, but who were now seen by some elements of society as enemies of Britain. My father spoke of the occasion when he and Kalistenis' sons had to arm themselves with pieces of wood and knives just to be able to make it out of the estate where they were living in Kings Cross. They could only come and go in a group for mutual protection, otherwise they would have become the easy prey of the marauding teddy boys.

"The teddy boys gathered at the entrance to the flats. Most of them were only sixteen or seventeen-year-olds. They were silly boys trying to behave as if they were tough guys…like in the films. They didn't really understand the seriousness of what they were doing. They probably enjoyed wearing their teddy boy clothes or 'togs' as they would refer to them and combing their hair in an Elvis Presley style. They used to loiter around and make a lot of noise, but they were not a great threat. If their mothers knew where they were and what they were doing, they would have been in trouble for sure. It was only when they were joined by two or three older thugs who could be armed that things became really serious. I think they were influenced by right wing extremists who hated us and other foreign people who tried to become popular by blaming immigrants for everything that was wrong in society. Their tactics were usually to attack a person on their own or perhaps two people walking together. Their gang, five or six in number, often beat their victim severely so that he needed to go to hospital. On rare occasions, people died. The police always arrived too late to apprehend anyone involved in the attack. They hit and run! Within a week or two, they came back, loitering around, making a great deal of noise and looking for their next victim. There were four of us: Kalistenis' three sons and me. They made remarks at us on our way in and out of the estate but there were enough of us to make them think twice before attacking. We had to be very careful not to be caught alone by these thugs, otherwise it would have been very dangerous."

Once when Father was relating this particular story, I asked him why he stayed in England if life was so difficult.

"I stayed because I had nothing to go back for. I had no work, no money and no house. I was desperate. The friends and companions were always fun to be with, but they could not feed you and your children or pay your bills or let you sleep in their house. Above all, you need work to earn money. Without this, you are lost and England has mountains of work. You can work for the rest of your life and you will still have more work if you want it. That is why I have stayed here. That is why I think that England is a great place… I work, and I have money to live and I don't have to ask for any favours from anyone!"

"What about the teddy boys?" I asked.

"The teddy boys were just a passing phase. The racists are always there and they are in every country. They are even in Cyprus where the Greek Cypriot racists teach their children to hate Turkish Cypriots and the Turkish Cypriot racists teach their children to hate the Greek Cypriots. Racists are everywhere and if you give them a chance, they can destroy democracy. In England, there are powerful people who will not let this happen. They are the same people who beat Hitler and the Nazis and they are not about to let some racist thugs destroy the democracy of this country. But Cyprus is another matter."

He reflected and spoke more slowly and more sadly because he was thinking of his homeland.

"Even though the Greek and Turkish Cypriot people are very alike, they have been brainwashed into thinking that they are enemies with each other and I don't think we have anyone who is smart enough or courageous enough to stand up to the racists in Cyprus. One day, I really think they will destroy the whole island unless people begin to understand how evil this racism really is."

Despite his lack of education and some of his wayward habits, Father had political ideas. He often spoke about how Greek and Turkish Cypriot workers had more in common with each other than with the rich elite from their own communities. He was very conscious about how working-class people had to labour extremely hard while the rich got richer.

"It doesn't matter where you are, it could be Cyprus or England or America. The working people get peanuts while the rich live in luxury."

Father was a socialist because he had always been one of the millions who worked and got very little in return. He was a member of the A.K.E.L.[1] the communist party of Cyprus. He attended meetings and gave his support because he felt that it was the only political organisation on the island that wanted to help the ordinary, working people. He hated nationalism and racism because it divided working people and prevented workers from bettering themselves. It was also the only political party that promoted peace and reconciliation between Greek Cypriots and Turkish Cypriots.

Father had some sound ideas in his head, and it was when he spoke with such faith and optimism, despite so many challenges and problems in his life, that I felt very proud of him.

In London, the racist attacks grew in intensity and by the summer of 1958, the West Indians living in Notting Hill were deliberately targeted by teddy boys and right wing racist thugs whose slogan was 'keep Britain white'. Eventually, the sustained intimidation and attacks led to the Notting Hill riots[2] in which West Indians confronted the teddy boys on the streets of that area. Some years later, gangs of skinheads subjected the Bangladeshi community of Brick Lane to violence and abuse.[3] Before these, more recent arrivals to the shores of the British Isles, it was the Jews who had sought sanctuary from the pogroms of central and Eastern Europe, who in the 1930s had to face Mosley[4] and his Fascist thugs dressed in black shirts in imitation of their role models, the Italian fascisti and the German Nazis.

Even with an optimistic outlook, it took a while for Britain's new people to be accepted as citizens and for the new people to acquire the understanding of 'Britishness' that enabled them to become, in their own right, British people. This eventually happened, but it was then a distant goal that neither British people, nor the immigrants were aware of at that time. It was a gradual process of nation building; the absorbing of new people into the fabric of British society. It was bringing people of diverse backgrounds together, respecting each other's culture, being united, having equal rights before the law, working and living in one united community. The teddy boys and the Notting Hill riots, the attacks by skinhead National Front[5] supporters on the Bengalis of the East End and the provocative demagogy of Enoch Powell[6] represented those elements that rejected a society that could include people of different races, colour and creed but who failed to prevent it from happening.

Opposed to the racists was the concept of democracy held by reasonable people that all citizens are equal. Equality and equal opportunities for all groups in society was something that had to be worked on and achieved. It didn't happen on its own. There were people and politicians in England who were determined that it should happen. Most politicians understood that it was important for people in the United Kingdom to be treated with equality, dignity and they expressed this view in political debates. More marvellous then this, however, was the reaction of the ordinary British people, who over a period of time, showed that they could progress from the suspicion and sometimes hostility towards immigrants of the 1950s and 1960s to the understanding and appreciation of people from diverse backgrounds in this present time. Racism isn't totally defeated, the racists are still lurking, but people are more aware of how negative and evil it can be. Time, experience and goodwill, it seems, are good teachers.

At the end of his anecdotes about the teddy boy thugs, Father had the habit of pausing to reflect upon what he had said. Perhaps, as people sometimes do, he thought and relived those experiences in his life and tried to put them into some kind of perspective:

"Most of the teddy boys were just silly, misguided teenagers. They were impressionable and behaved without thinking. Generally, people were fair. You encountered these people in the street and in the work place. They were often busy getting on with their own lives, they had their own concerns and troubles. Usually, they just passed you by without so much as a glance in your direction. The nice thing about the English is that they mind their own business most of the time and they expect you to do the same."

~

On rare occasions, Father managed to post some money to assist Mother with her preparations for us to join him in England. He described the life and the conditions that he had found. He expressed his admiration for the new-found land, for that is what England was felt to be and his hopes for the future.

London,
December, 1956.
Beloved wife,
First, may I enquire regarding your health and the health of our children. I pray to God that you are all well. Praise be to God that I am well and able to work every day and believe me, I am working day and night. My place of work is a factory that produces sausages and when you come to England there will be a job for you too. It is a huge factory full of machines. We have to wear special white overalls for hygiene. We look like doctors. My job is to fill the mixing machine with the meat for

sausages. I put in a huge amount of mincemeat that has been specially prepared. The machine turns this into sausages. You put the meat in from the top and the sausages come out from the bottom. The factory makes thousands of sausages every day.

At the moment, I am living with our former neighbours from Cyprus, Prokopis and Kalisteni. They are good people and we try to support each other. They are just the same as they were in Cyprus. One day, they are like lovebirds, and the next day, they are screaming and shouting at each other, especially if Prokopis makes a visit to a pub where he drinks before he comes home.

It has been very difficult to save money because here in England, even though you have the chance to work and earn money, everything is very expensive and all the money soon disappears. You just would not believe how much it costs to buy a packet of cigarettes. It is three times what they cost in Cyprus.

I have saved some money and I am able to send you £20 to help you with the preparation for your journey to England. Book immediately and without hesitation. I have already spoken to a certain Cypriot who has a large house and he is prepared to rent us two rooms and a kitchen. There is a good school nearby for Fotaki and also a secondary school for Kika because children must go to school until the age of fifteen. Everything will be ready by the time that you and the children arrive. We will work very hard and we will build our lives again.

London is a great and wonderful city. It is a huge place with thousands of streets with buildings stuck together on either side. Something you can hardly believe even with your own eyes are the hundreds of trains that travel under the ground all day long, carrying millions of people to work every day. There are really great opportunities in England and I know things will be better for all of us.

I miss you and the children, kiss them for me. That is all I have to say at this time,

Your husband,

Loizos.

Immigrants like my father, who had made the journey to England or to the United States or perhaps to Australia, did so with the intention of helping those who were left behind, usually the wives and children. In many cases, money was sent to help maintain the families, paying for a son's secondary education or for medicine for elderly parents. Often, as in our story, the husband would be followed to the new land by the wife and the children. The journey was always the first step, the beginning of the dream to build a better life, to have some better expectations on what the future would be like.

1. A.K.E.L. – Progressive Party of Working People. Greek: Anorthotiko Komma Ergazomenou. Turkish: Emekci Halkin Ilerici Partisi.

2. Notting Hill Riots – Many people from the Caribbean had settled in the Notting Hill area which in the fifties had been run down and crime infested. The people from the Caribbean had arrived through the encouragement of the British Government because of the need for cheap labour in the growing British economy. In Notting Hill, there was an increasing competition for housing between black and white families that had led to hostile feelings which were further aggravated by teddy boys, white working-class youths who often exhibited a racist attitude towards back people. Further, the Union for British Freedom and Sir Oswald Mosley, the leader of the British Union of Fascists was trying to make a comeback in popularity after his dismal failure and incarceration during the war years. He had established himself in Notting Hill with the intention of causing confrontation and trouble. By 24th August, 1958, there was series of violence in the streets of Notting Hill. It had been caused mainly by white youths in their hundreds, openly attacking members of the Caribbean community. The police and government, not wishing to reveal the truth that racial hatred had degenerated into open conflict on the streets of London, attributed the violence to hooligans both black and white. "The Home Office Cover Up of Notting Hill's Race Riots." Ian Barrel, The Independent. August, 2003. "After 44 years, Secret Papers Reveal Truth About Five Nights of Violence in Notting Hill." Alan Travis. *The Guardian* August, 2002.

3. Brick Lane Riots. Before the riots of 1978 had occurred, there had been harassment and attacks on people of the Bengali community who lived around the area of Brick Lane. The murder of Altab Ali, a young Bengali man on his way home from work, sparked the demonstrations and protests that followed. It was felt that the tactics of the racists and the presence of the National Front had to be challenged. As if adding fuel to the fire, the proposals of the GLC on June 4th, to house exclusively Bengalis in particular blocks of flat, led to an explosive situation. Up to one hundred and fifty white youths rampaged through Brick Lane throwing brick, bottles and concrete slabs. In due course, however, the National Front was

forced out of the area. "Brick Lane1978. The Events and Their Significance." Kenneth Leech, 2014.

4. Mosley was leader of the British Union of Fascists which he founded in 1932. The B.U.F. was successfully challenged in the streets of the East End of London when the local residents, particularly on the 4th of October, 1935, confronted and prevented them from marching through the area. This event came to be known as the Battle of Cable Street. When asked what changes he would make to the immigration laws of alien races into Great Britain, his reply was an ominous and threatening, "All immigration will be stopped. Britain for the British is our motto and all of Britain is required for the British. Further, all foreigners who have been naturalised will be deported unless they have proved themselves valuable citizens of Great Britain." In 1940, Mosley was interned and was never again to play any significant role in British politics.
The Life and Times of Sir Oswald Mosley and the British Union of Fascists.
Holocaust Education and Archive Research Team. Editor Carmilo Lisociotto H.E.A.R.T. 2010.

5. The National Front was founded by A. K. Chesterton in 1967. Its founding ideology was based on extreme nationalism that promoted the repatriation of immigrants. It was never to enjoy any success in national politics or elections. "N. F: History of the far right in Britain." James Kirkup. 22nd October, 2009.

6. Enoch Powell was a British politician who used demagogy to gain the interest of the British public. He presented immigration to Britain, particularly from the New Commonwealth, as an existential threat to Britain. In his so-called 'Rivers of Blood' speech that he delivered to a Conservative Association meeting in Birmingham on 20th April, 1968, he describes how the influx of black and Asian people would lead to a cataclysmic future: "As I look ahead, I am filled with foreboding; Like the Roman, I see the River Tiber foaming with much blood." *The Telegraph*, 6th November, 2007.

The Departure

By 1957, Mother had managed to save enough money and with the small amount sent by Father, she was able to pay for our passage to England. We booked our passage through one of the few travel agents of that time. 'Patsalidis' had a reliable reputation. We would travel by ship from Larnaca to Genoa in Italy and from there, by overnight train to Calais. We would cross the English Channel to Dover and then complete our journey by train to Victoria Station.

My mother felt rather nervous at the thought of what was to her a long and complicated journey with two small children. Having to go by ship across the seas and trains that travel through countries where the people spoke in strange languages seemed very daunting to her. She had never travelled by ship or train before. She had never left the shores of her native island, and so the prospect of what appeared to her an epic journey into very unfamiliar territory left her feeling somewhat anxious and a little nervous.

"Mr Patsalidis, it seems a very long way and we don't speak their languages, I will be lost with my children."

Mr Patsalidis was a thin, wiry man in his late thirties. He was dressed in a brown summer suit and wore an eye-catching, shiny yellow tie. He sat on a wooden chair behind his desk that was covered with some neat piles of papers. He constantly made sharp, quick movements that are typical of people who are unable to relax and who think that they should busily be getting on with things. He was reassuring because he had heard such doubts before.

"Don't worry, Mrs Loizou, there will be other people with you going the same way. Follow them and show your documents."

He smiled as he spoke to my mother who remained unconvinced by his smooth talking. Seeing her reluctance, he felt that he needed to gently encourage her.

"You know, Mrs Loizou, that we have very few tickets at the moment for the sea and train passage. There is a very high demand, half of Cyprus wants to go to England! We Cypriots are the most confused people on this earth. First, we want the British to leave Cyprus and then half of Cyprus wants to go to live in their country! I just don't know what is going on in our muddled brains!" he said this in a half-serious, half-joking manner, smiling at his own, very truthful observation.

"The ship belongs to the Arsa Line and they are safe and reliable. I've used them many times before. If you don't take these tickets now, it will be sometime before I will be able to offer this journey so cheaply."

At the thought of further delay to our plans, Mother relented. "We will book the tickets now and thank you, Mr Patsalidis."

It was as if Mother had brushed her worries and doubts to one side and was ready to step into the unknown. It was one of those moments in which the decision taken would have enormous repercussions on our lives. As if Mr Patsalidis realised the significance of the moment and how important it was for Mother, he looked at her and at my sister and me in silence for a second or two and smiled again with an expression of understanding, as if he was able to see into the future.

"You will be fine, Mrs Loizou, you will be fine."

The day of our departure was drenched in brilliant winter sunshine that gave the day a false sense of joy. Everything seemed in high definition, almost exaggerated, as friends and family gathered at our baranga. They had come to say goodbye. My uncles Mihalis and Fotis with Mother's sisters, their wives, Aunt Filou and Aunt Christinou. They had come with their children from Sotira to bid us farewell and to wish us success on our venture. Aunt Martha and her children with my grandparents, Kyros and Kyriacou, came from Stylloi. It was a family gathering to mark a special event. Such gatherings occurred to celebrate a birth or a wedding, to mourn the passing away of a loved one. This gathering was to mark the day of our departure to another land. Our relatives had come to bid us farewell.

In contrast to the cheerfulness of the morning sunshine, my grandparents looked decidedly unhappy. They could not bear the thought that one of their dear daughters was about to leave with two of their beloved grandchildren, perhaps never to be seen by them again, for who can say how life will evolve and what unforeseen circumstances may arise on life's journey. They were old and felt very uncertain about Mother's decision to go.

The talking continued. Adults drank sweet Cyprus coffee in the shade cast by the pines and oleanders in the courtyard of the baranga. There were children playing, running around and kicking up dust from the dry soil. There was laughter, encouragement and loud conversation. But the noise and light heartedness was artificial and only thinly disguised the fears and anxieties which were particularly felt by my grandparents. They knew that departure from the homeland was more permanent and often irreversible.

There had been others who had gone to England or America; the years had passed by, but they were never to return. Grandmother could no longer hold back her concerns. There was an outpouring of hot tears that ran from her weather worn face. The chatter of adults and the children's games slowly ceased as everyone present and with now, serious, melancholic expressions, turned their gaze towards the old matriarch who sat in the middle of her large family. She adjusted her *kouroukla*, pulling it slightly lower over her forehead as if to make the point that for her this was an important and formal occasion, an occasion full of panic, pain and pathos. She pleaded with my mother not to go. She wanted to persuade, to warn, to do everything in her power, even at the last minute, even at the eleventh hour, to change Mother's mind, to dissuade her from leaving Cyprus. She was determined not to let her daughter and grandchildren go to some unknown place; she was going to use every argument and every reason to change her daughter's mind.

"You will go to a far-off land full of strangers, the bread of exile is bitter. Who knows what misfortunes await you…alone with your little children and an unreliable husband who will betray you; to whom will you turn?"

Her voice was filled with emotion. The tears began to flow again. Grandmother mourned as if it was a funeral as she continued her arguments against the journey. It was like a scene from a Greek Tragedy.

"You will be alone and isolated. At least here you are with people who love and care for you. In a foreign land, who is going to look at you in your hour of need? Who is going to knock at your door to offer you even a crust of bread? Have you forgotten how your dear husband dragged you from Sotira to Stylloi and now from Varosi to only God knows where? Do not be fooled by him, he will never change, he will always betray you! And where is this London? It is on the other side of the world and whoever is foolish enough to go there, never returns. How cruel that you are going to take my grandchildren away from me…"

Her tirade came to a sudden end. Grandmother's words had cut to the bone. She didn't care whether her words were hurtful or offensive. She felt that she was speaking the truth in an attempt to safeguard her daughter and grandchildren. She was determined that even at the last moment before the departure, she would prevent Mother from committing what she believed to be the greatest mistake of her life.

Mother was moved by such an emotional expression of feelings but she managed to retain her composure and answered in a kindly, respectful manner. She took her mother's hand, looked into her dark eyes, now reddened by her tears and spoke to her gently but with conviction.

"Mother, I must go to my husband; things will be better. What can we do here for our children? They cannot eat the air. The young women grow old before their time and the young men waste their lives in listless unemployment. They become angry because they have no future. Do not worry mother, it is for the best."

"But what about my grandchildren, what is going to happen to them? When will I see my little pretty birds again?" she continued to weep.

"Oh, Mother, don't cry for the children. If they stay here, they will grow up poor without a real chance in life; in England, they will go to school, they will have opportunities to become something wonderful and my husband and I will be able to work, we will have a home, a proper home, not a baranga like we have now. Our country is beautiful but for poor people like us, the life is too hard!"

"Are you certain that you can trust Loizo. How many times has he let you down? How many times did he say one thing then did the opposite?"

Grandmother would have said anything to change mother's mind.

"He has learnt from his mistakes," answered Mother defensively, "and in his letters, he promises that we will build a better life than what we had here. I have to trust what he says because he is my husband and the father of my children; one more thing, Mother, you know how scandalous Cypriots can be about a woman without a husband. They will start malicious rumours that I sleep with other men and very soon, I will have a reputation of being worse than a prostitute. Do you want that to happen to me? No, Mother, I cannot permit such a thing to happen."

Mother had spoken with passion. It was an emotional outburst that she needed to express as if she was somehow justifying her actions not only to others, but also to herself. Mother's dramatic proclamation did not impress Grandmother who then just busied herself with the children, trying very hard for my mother's sake to weep no more. There were times, some very hard times, however, in the following months and years, when Mother expressed her feeling that she should have listened to Grandmother's advice.

Just before we boarded the mini-bus for Larnaca, we all gathered close together in a group for a photograph. At the front, seated were my grandparents and I sat between them. Behind us, arranged in two lines were my uncles and aunts. Many years later when I visited Cyprus, I saw this photograph for the first time on the wall of my Aunt Eleni's living room. The photograph held my attention not only because I saw myself as a little boy surrounded by the people who loved me, but because the photograph had captured the moment after which the familiar life, that could have been, was to change for an unpredictable experience. The photograph captured the moment of sadness of those who were left behind; it showed the relationship that would imminently be severed but also of the hope of a better future for those who were leaving.

The suitcases were then hoisted onto the roof rack of the old, rusting minibus. They contained all our belongings. Mother was careful to pack 'malina' woollen sheets for the cold English climate. These sheets had been woven at home by my grandmother who worried that we would not be warm enough in the winter months ahead. She had also packed towels, table cloths, knives and forks, some pots and pans beside our ordinary clothes. She had put into those suitcases as much of her household belongings as possible for her new home in England. Mother had also shared out between her sisters other household possessions that she could not take with us. She gave them pots and pans of good quality, a fine, solid oak dining table with some chairs and an iron bed with a comfortable mattress. Many years after when I visited my aunties, they pointed to these things and commented on how generous my mother had been.

"This table and this iron bed belonged to your mother, Fotaki, and she kindly gave them to us."

Another aunt perhaps added some explanation on how it came about that she had acquired mother's household items,

"She gave me those plates with a fine glaze and the heavy cooking pots because you were going to England and she had no means by which to take them with her."

My aunts had always been kind and religious women, but on those occasions when my mother's things were displayed before me, I was overcome with the uncomfortable feeling that my aunts had been happy to benefit from our departure to England. Perhaps, I was wrong about this and I was only disturbed with the thought that those things made us into merely a memory in the place where we should have had a real existence; but this was not something that I dwelt on for too long because the past is beyond our ability to alter, not that I wanted to change it because our lives in our new-found land, though not without its own problems, were full of opportunities, enriched and fulfilling.

Just before we boarded the minibus, my sister's best friends came to say good-bye. It was Eve, who was my sister's closest and dearest friend. Later, in England, my sister often showed the photograph of Eve and always commented that she was indeed a very beautiful girl, a charming person and a dear friend. Eve's brother was Kokos. He was a fine, handsome young man who had warm feelings for my sister and had hoped one day to make her his wife. After some years we had been in England, Kokos suddenly and unexpectedly turned up from nowhere, seeking my sister. He was shocked and upset to discover that she had become engaged to someone else and he left our house looking bewildered and despondent.

Eventually, after years of being in England and because of the upheavals of 1974 in Cyprus, contact with such friends was lost. Information about old acquaintances was sometimes discovered through a chance meeting with a common friend who explained and told the story of what may have happened to those who were once close, with whom life would have been shared but with whom the bonds were severed by the decision to go far away across the sea to another land.

We eventually boarded the old rusting minibus. From the windows, we looked out at the scene. We looked at the baranga with its walls of peeling paint, its leaking roof and windows that did not close properly. This had been our home. The warm, winter sunshine, the azure dome of the sky and the tranquil, timeless, solitary caique that could be seen from where we were, sailing below the horizon in a sparkling sea was not enough to lighten the sombre mood. With tears and with brave smiles, we waved good-bye to friends and family. The driver revved up the engine and with a sudden jerk, the first steps of the journey were taken. The minibus slowly wove its way through the narrow streets of Varosi. In the centre of the town, the people were hurrying hither and thither. Housewives were on their way to the pantopoulion, the municipal market, to buy the provisions for the day. Men walked alone, sometimes smoking a cigarette or in pairs talking, on their way to work. Children walked in twos or in small groups, teasing and shouting, joking with each other, running around tirelessly on their way to school. On this day, however, I was not on my way to school. I was on my way to England. This was a momentous day for me, one that would determine the kind of person that I would become.

Making our way out of the city, we passed the old Venetian walls and took the road in the direction of Larnaca from where we intended to embark on a ship of the Arsa Line for Genoa in Italy, our first port of call. Little did we know then that the passing of time and the fortunes of war would mean that even up to this present moment, we are prevented from returning to the beloved city of Evagoras, Varosi, our home town, the place of my earliest memories, the place where I first went to school, where I played on its golden beach and where I first began to have a sense of myself.

Today it is a ghost town, its citizens have been scattered, victims of a merciless invasion, forbidden to return to their homes by a foreign occupation army. There is also the cruel and unjust threat that the town could be given to colonists for resettlement while the true owners are deprived of the homes that they had built with their own labour. This ghost town, once full of life and activity and hope, remains since 1974, a symbol of man's inhumanity to man.[1]

1. Ghost town – On 15th of July, the anti-Makarios coup d'état was launched by the Greek officers who controlled the Cyprus National Guard with the aim of achieving Enosis, union with Greece. Turkey of course, strongly opposed such a move and citing the rights of intervention granted to her by the 1960 Article 2 of the Treaty of Guarantee, on the 20th of July, 1974, launched an invasion of the island to protect the Turkish Cypriots and to safeguard its interests. During the days following the invasion, Greek Cypriots who were in the way of the advancing Turkish forces had to flee for their safety. This included the 40,000 citizens of Varosi who were driven out of their town by the onslaught of the Turkish Army who then declared the town a military area and prevented its rightful and legitimate citizens from returning to their homes.

The Journey

There was hardly any traffic on the road. The minibus occasionally overtook a lonely cyclist or slowed down as it carefully went by a 'carretta', a two-wheeled cart used by farmers and usually drawn by a single horse. The countryside seemed soothing and still, silent like a painting of an Italian medieval landscape. In the distance, we observed some figures that seemed to be painted on a canvas. The white, winter, fluffy clouds contrasted sharply with the unspoilt blue of the Mediterranean sky.

The first indication that our bus journey was almost complete was when we saw the Salt Lake. The rain had been heavy at the beginning of that winter and the lake which was always dry in the summer months was now almost overflowing. It was now so tranquil; its surface was like a mesmerising mirror reflecting the morning light. There were flocks of wild birds that had migrated from Europe on their way to Africa, basking and feeding in its warm waters. Occasionally, the movement of the wild fowl caused ripples that extended here and there on the surface of the translucent waters of the lake and seemed to journey outwards until they disappeared from view.

On the opposite side, the far bank was covered with green shrubs and exotic palm trees. Amongst the deep green branches of the palm trees, almost hidden, we caught sight of the Tekke of Hala Sultan, the resting place of the Prophet's relative Oum Haram, who according to history during the time of the Arab invasions of the 7th century, had fallen from her horse and had died there. The image of the trees and the Tekke was reflected onto the lake as were the white clouds and the blue sky from above. It was as if there were two identical parallel worlds side by side. One above and one below the waters of the lake. This magical impression of the Tekke seemed to come straight out of the stories of the *Arabian Nights*.

In the years to come, I nostalgically recalled this scene in my mind's eye when thinking of my distant homeland. The gentle warmth of its winter sun, the purity of its air and the unforgettable landscape of its plains, hills and mountainside, its sleepy villages and towns had deeply stimulated my senses and impressed my imagination. It was a place of duality, where the church and mosque stood side by side, where the Christian and Moslems lived as neighbours, where, as people, they shared common aspirations and hopes. For many years in the lives of the people of Cyprus, this is how it had been, but it was not to endure.

The bus soon arrived at the port, outside the point of embarkation. As we alighted from the bus, a flock of birds swirled three times above the port and then flew off towards the open sea. They were migratory birds moving compulsively towards new destinations, to build new nests in far off places. They flew swiftly, slicing through the air, without hesitation or fear. They flew with a purpose and a certainty and a determination and without the need to look back.

We stood on the quay, looking out at the ship that was anchored some distance from the shore. There were at least twenty other people who were also waiting to embark. There were men who were standing alone, with one or two suitcases beside them; perhaps some were single men without wives or children who were intent on finding their fortune. Others might have been bread winners with families to think about, who wanted to work hard to provide a better life for them. And there must have been amongst them those who were running away from the people they had known, the familiar streets of their city where the experience had become uncomfortable for them. They might have had a sense of failure and the desire to begin again, to turn the page, to start a new chapter. There were some couples who were holding hands tightly in case the one would depart on the waiting ship without the other. There were children of various ages for whom the journey ahead was like a great adventure. They were excited and were not perturbed for the moment about leaving anyone behind or when they would see their homeland again. Whatever their reasons for leaving their place of birth, whatever their feelings at that important juncture in their lives, whatever their fears for the future, they all waited patiently for their turn to be transported to the waiting ship.

The port of Larnaca in those days was not sufficiently deep to allow ships to dock within it. Our several suitcases were loaded onto a small craft and then we also boarded. The sea was calm and turquoise blue. When we had settled, the engine was started up and the boat quickly cut through the clean water while its skipper, a stout, unshaven, sunburnt man whistled and spoke in a loud voice.

"Don't be afraid, you're safe with me. So, you are going to England! You'll all be rich very quickly! You'll be back before you know it with your pockets full of money! You will build palaces and live like the pashas!"

He laughed loudly at his own irony while his passengers uncomfortably looked down at the depth of the water and at how his little boat was heavily overloaded.

"Be careful, drive the boat smoothly, we don't want to be drowned before we have even left Cyprus!" called out a young passenger with a half-smile on his face.

"Young man," retorted the unshaven skipper of the boat in a humorous tone and with a broad grin on his face, "you are in the hands of Sener Moustafa and with Allah's help, I will never let you down!"

We all laughed at the exchange of words between the young passenger and the old skipper. The bantering had released the tension that we had felt at the point of embarkation.

Soon, we came by the side of the ship and stopped where a rope and wooden staircase had been lowered to enable us to embark. We made our way on board and some sailors brought on our luggage. The ship was crowded with Cypriots who had boarded before us. Mr Patsalides was speaking the truth when he said that we would not be alone on this journey. As we stood on the deck, we noticed that the smoke from the two funnels of the ship had increased and there was the rumble of the engines from somewhere inside the depths of the vessel. Then it began to move, first very slowly, and then gradually with greater speed. As I stood on the deck peering out over the railings, momentarily it seemed to me that the land was moving and that the ship was static. When I regained my equilibrium, I could see that the ship had begun its journey. As the ship gathered speed, the coast of beloved Cyprus grew smaller and smaller. I kept my eyes on the ever-diminishing land until it was just a spot on the distant horizon. I gazed and gazed, straining my eyes until the island was finally out of sight. At that moment, a sudden sadness overcame me. It was as if something truly important, something that I really held dear in my heart, something that I would really miss, an important part of myself, was now gone. As a child, I could not articulate such feelings but even at a tender age, that is how I felt. It was goodbye, I understood, to my humble but much loved home; to the friends with whom I fought and played; the beach of Varosi with its golden, hot sand; it was farewell to my wonderful grandmother who had told me stories so full of life's meaning, to my brooding, silent Grandfather who loved us immensely; to my cousins who always welcomed us to the village with huge smiles; it was adieu to uncles and aunties who supported and cared for us. It was goodbye to all of them.

At night, the passengers crowded on the decks; they took out blankets and made sleeping arrangements under the Mediterranean night sky. The air was fresh and cool, and the firmament was lit up by constellations of stars. The people were joyful, as people often are when they set out on long journeys. They were full of hope and optimism for the future. They talked, laughed and engaged in serious conversations. Some were delighted to meet up with acquaintances, friends or relatives, all making the same journey. There was innocence and naivety in the expectations of these people. Many were from villages. They were shepherds or farmers, skilled in animal husbandry or ploughing, planting, irrigating crops, reaping the seasonal fruits of the soil. Those from towns were small traders with crafts: a tailor, a shoemaker, a carpenter or a barber. All were poor, and all were immigrating for a better future. Their aim was to build something, to achieve, to find opportunities. All had a dream and a desire to improve themselves. There were many voices spoken by different individuals, but it was always the same theme.

"I have three daughters who need a dowry. In England, I can earn enough money to provide them with all they need."

"My son is a very bright boy. I will work for a few years so that he can go to the gymnasium. I will send them money. My cousin has a restaurant in London and I can work for him."

"I'm a labourer. I've heard that in England you can get a fair wage for the work that you do. In Cyprus, you can't get anywhere unless you have the right contacts."

"I am going to work very hard. I want to buy a house and have my own business."

Their conversation endured well into the night until they were exhausted and one by one, they succumbed to sleep. For them, England was the promised land: a land of hope, a land at the end of the rainbow, a land flowing with milk and honey and they were the Hebrews crossing the Red Sea in search for the fulfilment of hope. They needed to believe that the future held something good, something that would lighten their suffering and alleviate their poverty. And for the majority, England would provide some realisation of their dreams. Whatever the distant outcome, the experience which began on that ship sailing through the night would change their lives in many unforeseen ways. The immigrants were leaving behind an ancient land and even these simple people were full of its history; they knew its culture and practised its traditions. They breathed, spoke and felt their identity. They were Cypriots, God fearing, Christian and Moslem, people who laboured from dawn to dusk to build better lives. Their voices from the past still endure in the tales told about the exodus from the old homeland and are repeated by their descendants in memory of that journey so long ago.

We too met acquaintances and friends. George, my father's first cousin, was also travelling to England. He was a slender man in his early thirties. He had brown curly hair that was neatly cut and combed back to expose a broad forehead. His expression was serious but he had a friendly and polite manner. He showed great respect for family ties and it was our good fortune that through coincidence, he was travelling with us. He proved to be our constant friend and helper. When my mother often repeated her thanks and expressed her gratitude to him for his assistance, he would smile and modestly say,

"It is for my relatives, we are one family, we are one blood." He was a shy person, but he was always with us, lifting or carrying some of our luggage or looking out for our safety, making certain that we were never in any kind of danger.

I was beginning to enjoy the journey; I was six years old and I had never been on a ship before. When I looked at the bow of the ship, how it sliced its way through the water, I was filled with excitement. On that very first day of our journey, we sighted dolphins swimming by the side and ahead of the ship, darting through the water, leaping and diving in and out of the sea. In my amazement, I ran hither and thither to keep sight of them. My mother became so alarmed that I might somehow fall off the ship or have an accident that she forced me to be with her at all times. I felt restricted and my fun was again being spoilt. She gripped me firmly by the hand and would not let me out of her sight. I stood next to her with a miserable expression on my face, feeling glum and sad at the level of motherly control I had to endure. Life seemed so very unfair!

On the second day of our journey, we sailed north of the island of Crete and onwards towards Italy. The adults passed most of their time talking or perhaps resting in their cabins. There was actually little to do because, though the ship was transporting passengers, it was also a cargo ship engaged mainly for the purpose of carrying goods and therefore afforded little comfort to its passengers. For me, however, it was a magnificent sailing ship that was carrying me, as I imagined, on some great adventure and I pondered in my childish imagination whether we would stop on the island of the Cyclopes or perhaps encounter the Sirens[1] with their mesmerising songs who, if we were not careful, would cause our ship to be wrecked against the rocks. I was once again with my greatest hero, the cunning and wise Odysseus, King of Ithaka, sacker of cities, sailing across the wine dark sea, looking for adventure. However, Mother was always not far behind and always ready to bring me back to reality.

On the third day of our journey, we disembarked at Genoa. Italy was the first foreign country that we had ever been to and Genoa was like no other place that we had ever seen before. There were masses of people everywhere you looked. Some were dressed in very fashionable clothes, walking in a kind of slow promenade, as if inviting on lookers to note their importance, while others busily went about their affairs and all the time, we could hear people engaging in the musical Italian tongue. Some were speaking in a loud and musical tone as they walked along, others were calling out to each other, children laughed and talked at the same time. The sound of this language impressed and entertained us with its operatic and rhythmic qualities. Mother was also very impressed with the Italian sense of style and the animated manner of the Italians. These Europeans were so different from the English people with their blue eyes, blond hair, fair skin that sunburnt so easily under the Cyprus sun, that she had worked with at Four Miles. In contrast, the Italians with their dark hair and olive skin, their loud voices and body language seemed familiar people. She felt their warmth and could relate to them as if they were rediscovered, distant relatives.

"What beautiful buildings and the people seem to be so kind," Mother occasionally uttered, but her favourable opinion of Italy and the Italians was not destined to endure for any length of time: we had some spare time before our train was due to leave and so we went for a walk in a park, close to the railway station from where we were to begin the second stage of our journey. Unknown to us, this particular park must have been a place for young lovers. After strolling for about five minutes, Mother could no longer ignore what she was seeing. There were young couples on park benches or lying on the grass, embracing and kissing. Some were passionately and erotically grasping each other. Mother could not believe her eyes. She had never seen such things going on in public in Cyprus; she felt that this was an outrage and a great sin.

"This place is Sodom and Gomorrah!" she cried. "God will punish this world!"

In a panic, she grabbed my hand, ordered my sister not to look at what was going on, covered her eyes with her other hand and with a feeling of righteous indignation, marched out of the park and straight to the train station, where we remained until it was time to board.

"What kind of a place is this," she repeated, "in which women allow men to embrace them in public as if they are in the marriage bed?"

Her opinion of Italy and the Italians had significantly changed from her first impressions.

~

For my mother and to the Cypriot women of her generation, the codes of dress and behaviour were dictated by what was thought to be standards of decency. A woman, they felt, should always be serious in public and not to be flirtatious or loud. She should be dressed modestly and wear little makeup if at all. The model of womanhood that was adhered to was that of a well-behaved daughter, a loyal wife or a noble mother. Anything else was considered unacceptable for an honourable family woman. Like my mother, most of the women journeying to England came from a deeply religious and conservative society in which roles were clearly defined; the boundaries between what was acceptable and unacceptable were drawn in clear, bold lines.

The Cypriot women of the 1950s worked extremely hard, cared for the house, brought up children and were subservient to their husbands. As single young women, their only prospect was marriage. The family began the preparations for the daughter's marriage even before adulthood. They provided a dowry, a house, furniture and sometimes land. It was unusual for women of the 1950s to be educated beyond primary school or to be a member of a profession, apart from perhaps school teaching.

My mother, like the other women of her time, spoke of these circumstances and conditions but these women also felt proud of their allotted place as wives, mothers and even as possessions of their husbands. Sometimes, they suffered the brutality of domestic violence inflicted upon them by husbands who felt they had a right to do this. Such men expressed the view that a woman should be kept in order. The Cypriot women of the 1950s did not openly rebel against such unfair attitudes. They accepted them because it had been like that for their grandmothers and mothers; such was life, they felt, and there wasn't anything that they could do about it and in most cases, it hardly ever occurred to them that there could be an alternative.

~

It was late afternoon when we boarded the train in Genoa. The suitcases were large and heavy, but thankfully George, my father's cousin, was there and was always willing to help. We soon found a compartment to ourselves, took out some bed clothes and blankets. The weather felt noticeably colder.

Eventually, the train set off and we were on our way, leaving the Mediterranean behind, heading towards France and beyond towards the English Channel. Mother was sitting between my sister and me. Opposite us, there was George. We talked and laughed; we were all very excited that we were at last well on our way. There was relief that we had completed the first part of our journey. We had crossed the sea and with each passing moment, we were travelling further and further from Cyprus and the world that was familiar to us. When would we again see its quiet, tranquil villages and sleepy little towns where the church bell tower stood side by side with the minaret? How were we going to feel when we would walk along unfamiliar roads, lost amongst people who spoke another language and who would look upon us with inquisitive glances?

The train seemed to be moving at a very high speed, faster than any vehicle that we had ever been on before. I could not sleep that night. I lay awake, filled with a strange joy, sensing that our journey was the prologue to great changes in our lives. As I closed my eyes to sleep, I felt the powerful, metallic heart of the train beating rhythmically, with enormous strength, like some magical dragon from the fairy tales, breathing fire as it journeyed through the cold darkness of the night, across deep valleys and through dark tunnels barrowed into mountains, crossing plains and forests, drawing ever closer to our destination.

By mid-morning of the next day, we had reached Calais. It was a rather cold and grey day with a drizzle that chilled us to the bone. There was no warm Mediterranean winter sunshine here! The demeanour of the people reflected the drabness of the environment; they were rather impersonal and to me, they looked rather sad. They hardly ever looked at each other and seemed to be in a great hurry. They had pale, unsmiling faces that seemed almost expressionless. We were quickly and efficiently transported from the station to the port where we boarded the ferry for Dover.

Once we had eventually managed to put our luggage in a secure place, we all went on deck to look at the scene. The sea had always been a familiar sight to us, but what we looked upon was something quite different from what we were used to. The sky was a dome of light grey with patches of white. There was hardly a horizon, the grey sky blended with a grey sea while the cold, fresh wind from the North Atlantic made our senses feel vibrant and alert, giving us a sense of wellbeing. We were further enthused when the greyness of the sky suddenly broke and in the distance, there appeared a patch of blue, through which bright silver rays from the hidden sun beamed down at the glittering sea. It was a tremendous, unfamiliar to us, panorama of delight. As we stood there on the deck of the cross-channel ferry, taking in the scene of sea and sky, Uncle George pointed to the white cliffs of Dover.

"There, there is England!" he exclaimed in a voice full of excitement.

The cliffs even from far away appeared to be gargantuan and majestic. They were like the walls of an impregnable fortress, guardians of England's liberty. I suppose we should have felt some kind of emotional excitement, but we were as yet unfamiliar with the stories and events that had made the scene of the white cliffs so special for the English people. In time, we would learn about their symbolic meaning and we would even learn the songs that romanticised them at a time of national crises and danger.

After disembarking, we were again efficiently conducted to our train for the last part of our journey. Once on the train, I sat by the side of the carriage window, looking out upon the scene. This was a neat, green land. The weather had changed since we were on board the ferry. It was still icy cold, but the sun was now shining in a blue sky with small, fluffy white clouds moving across it, like little sailing ships on a blue ocean. There was the greenest grass growing in field after field, full of flocks of fat wholesome, woolly sheep or herds of delightful, dappled black or dappled brown milk cows, dreamily grazing on the delicious, luxurious fodder.

At intervals, the train passed through towns with neat, two storey houses that were roofed with red or black tiles and where the steeples of little churches pointed high into the sky. Everything seemed so fresh, clean and crisp in the cold winter sunshine. We could see that the land was cultivated with tender loving care. Everything was neat and tidy, well-built and though old, was well maintained. This impression changed as we came closer to our final destination.

When we began to enter the great metropolis of London, the buildings were larger and the roads appeared more and more congested until all we could see were buildings, thousands of big and small smoking chimneys, roads and motorcars. The crisp, clean, green countryside could no longer be seen. Everything was brick and mortar, stained with the soot from the thousands of factories and coal burning fireplaces. Everything was iron: iron bridges spanning roads and rivers, iron railroads extending far and wide, iron motor cars crawling along busy roads. Our first impression of the megalopolis was that it was a city of iron, full of the smoke and noise of engines. Sometimes, as if to give relief from the hard grittiness of our first impression, we glanced at some grand old church with a high steeple or tower with a clock surrounded by pleasant houses. Occasionally, we caught sight of buildings that had been destroyed by the German Luftwaffe and had not yet been rebuilt. These blackened ruins seemed odd in the middle of a bustling metropolis and, of course, at that time, we had no idea that they were caused by the bombs that rained down on the people of London during the dark days of the Second World War.

I became increasingly excited when the train approached, crossed a gigantic bridge that spanned over the dark, fast flowing waters of the River Thames. I was awed by the dark deep waters of the river, how it flowed on into the horizon and how so many busy boats boisterously sailed up and down its waters. The defiant, majestic dome of Saint Paul's Cathedral that had withstood the bombardment of the Nazis and the Palace of West Minister standing along the margin of the river, majestically basked in the hazy, afternoon, winter sunshine.

The train was now moving very slowly as it began its approach to the station. On either side, there were countless shiny, smooth rail tracks that curved and crisscrossed each other like silver, slithering, metallic snakes, fading into the mammoth mouth of a dark tunnel. There were static trains that seemed to be resting after long journeys and trains slowly moving in the opposite direction to us, beginning their journeys to the different towns and cities of the land. Eventually, we entered a huge structure that was made from a web of steel and covered with glass panels. As I sat with my forehead against the carriage window, inspired and provoked by the brave new world that I was now entering, the train suddenly jerked and came to a complete standstill. At last, feeling tired but excited, we had arrived at London's Victoria Station.

There was a sudden commotion and movement of people in the carriages and along the corridor way. The doors of the carriages were flung open, the passengers began unloading their luggage from the racks above their heads and hauling them out of the compartments, into the corridor and with great labour, off the train and onto the platform. The spillage of people and luggage onto the platform, the noise of excitement from those who had just arrived, the deafening loud speaker announcements, the noise of metal on metal of other trains slowly leaving or coming to a standstill, created a cacophonous, chaotic arrival to the promised land. A sudden scream of desperation cut above the noise. A mother called out in a panic when she missed her child only to discover he was just standing a few feet behind her. In her relief, she hysterically shouted at the child, then hugged and kissed it. People busily checked to see if they had left anything behind on the train and then when all the luggage and the children were accounted for, they looked up at their surroundings, became conscious of the cold, lifted their coat collars against the chill air and as if realising for the first time that they were in an unfamiliar place, a foreign land, far from home, far from friends and neighbours with whom life had been shared, far from the familiar houses and roads of their towns and villages, they anxiously waited for their contact to meet with them.

1. The Sirens. They sang an enticing song to woo passing ships and sailors and to shipwreck them onto the rocks of their island. Odysseus having been forewarned of this danger orders his men to put bee's wax into their ears so that they could not be mesmerised by the songs of the Siren and to row past the island of the Sirens. Before this, however, he orders his men to tie him tightly to the mast so that he alone would be able to hear the magical song of the Sirens but be prevented from falling into their trap. Book 12.

100

Lines 200-258. *The Odyssey*. Homer. Translated by Robert Fitzgerald. Everyman.

London

"Is it here, Mama? Have we arrived? Is this London?" I called out excitedly to my mother, tugging at her sleeve.

"Will Papa be waiting?" asked my sister in an anxious manner.

"Yes, yes, of course, Papa will be waiting. Everything will be fine, we will soon see him," she answered in an uncertain voice.

Uncle George was meanwhile unloading the luggage from the train in his usual enthusiastic manner and even though he was a slender man, he never seemed to tire. We would often meet together in the future.

Father was waiting for us. We emerged from the train dishevelled and disorientated. He moved towards us. We could at last see him coming through the crowds. He had not changed at all. He seemed fresh and happy as he hugged Mother and then he kissed both my sister and me. I remember how he picked me up and looked at me in the eyes and said,

"You have really grown up, you are now such a big boy and you will soon go to your new English school."

All was joy, happiness and warm smiles at the realisation that at last we were together, reunited, one family again. There were tears of joy in my mother's eyes because after the long separation she stood again next to her husband. But she also felt, as she sometimes expressed in her conversations, that this reunion was at the cost of leaving other loved ones behind. There were her mother and father, there were her sisters and there was her country, the place where she had grown up and though her life there had been hard, it was still the place where she had been born, where she had grown to womanhood, had married and had become a mother, where all her friends were. When would she see again, all the people whom she loved? When would she again walk along the familiar roads of Varosi and see the sunrise and the sunset of her homeland?

We collected our luggage and made our way to the waiting car. The driver was a young man, Charalambos, who had been a neighbour in Cyprus. He was a familiar face in unfamiliar surroundings and his presence helped us not to feel overtly anxious because he was a young man who exuded confidence and goodwill. We were in good hands.

Surely, if Father and Charalambos had lived in this place for a whole year, then it couldn't be so bad.

We said goodbye to Uncle George who had been our greatest help throughout the journey. He was being met by someone else and had his own people waiting for him. We hugged and we kissed him because he was now not only a relative but also a very dear friend.

As we took our first steps through the station, we looked around us. This was the great Victoria Station, the first place that had made an impression on me in England. It was such a huge structure, bigger than any building we had ever seen before; it seemed awesome like a futuristic cavern or a gigantic cathedral crowded with people.

There was the constant sound and movement of the people who appeared energetic and full of purpose. Some were standing around in little groups looking excited, sometimes laughing in an exaggerated manner and constantly engaged in conversation; others stood on their own waiting for their trains. There were crowds of people who sat in cafés reading newspapers or talking with each other while the waiters and waitresses busied themselves with cleaning the tables, taking orders and serving an endless stream of customers. Another crowd of men and women stood below a huge board and with concentrated, upturned faces, reading the information on it. There were people of different races and some were dressed in colourful costumes from their native countries. There was a plethora of humanity, talking and laughing, walking slowly or rushing about, men and women young and old, rich or poor; they were a mass, a crowd composed of individuals going about their lives, each with their own private thoughts, a river of people that flowed in and out of the huge entrances and exits of the gigantic station and in the background, there was the constant sound of trains arriving and departing with their engines blowing steam and screaming mechanical sounds. There were the loud exclamations from porters pushing wheel burrows loaded with luggage, threading their way through the crowds.

"Mind yurr back! Look out, mind yurr back!" they exclaimed repeatedly.

I looked on with the wonder of a child. It was a new, unfamiliar, bewildering and confusing environment.

Charalambos, the driver, and my father carried the heavy luggage to save having to pay for a porter while mother, my sister and I carried some small bags. We slowly walked through the crowds of people and made our way out of the station through a massive arched gateway. We walked through it then down some steps and onto the bright, busy and bustling streets of London.

As we drove through the roads on our way to our new home, everything seemed to be illuminated in a festive manner. There were lights from every building and from every window. There were shops full of goods on display and, despite the exhaustion we felt, we looked on, feeling dazzled, dazzled and delighted. In fact, we had become so engrossed with the scenes unfolding before us that we had hardly noticed the severity of the cold. It was a frosty winter's evening and unlike anything we had previously experienced. The pavements were crowded with people. There were young couples walking hand in hand or in each other's arms, laughing and talking at the same time. Older ladies held their companions by the arm while walking in a more dignified manner. Children held on to their parents' hands, skipping along by their side with upturned faces, no doubt asking endless questions. Everybody wore long over coats, hats and scarves. Some were carrying umbrellas; they walked on the pavements with a brisk pace as if they all had somewhere very important to go. I looked on from the inside of the car not believing that I was in the same place as the pedestrians a few feet away. Perhaps, my mind had not yet adjusted to my new environment; perhaps I felt that if I blinked my eyes, I would find myself back at the beach in Varosi. Noticing how immersed I had become with the scene of our first view of London, my father spoke and smiled kindly.

"Fotaki, do you like London?"

It was the kind of question that you asked a child to prompt a conversation, but I was too mesmerised by the lights, the shop windows and the crowds of passing people to answer my father's question in any detail.

"I don't know," I answered in an inaudible voice.

Charalambos the driver chuckled, "Don't worry, he'll get used to it." Having been in London for longer than a year, Charalambos knew that it was a place that could easily become familiar, where you could easily work and make some money, where you could make friendships and get on with life.

My sister Kika had also been very quiet for a while. She had been analysing the way people dressed and how they appeared.

"The ladies look very glamorous. Their clothes are so beautiful and their hair and makeup are like the film stars in the *Romantzo* magazine…that is how I want to look when I am older."

My mother and father looked at each other, feeling both proud and amused. They had a daughter who was growing up and almost a woman.

Our car journey took us from Victoria Station to Dalston. East London had always been traditionally the first port of call for immigrants coming to London. It was now our turn, following in the footsteps of other immigrants who had lived there to take up residence for a while in that part of London.

Father had rented two rooms and a kitchen in a house that was owned by a Cypriot couple. The terraced, Victorian houses of Southgate Road N.1. seemed like castles to me. They had high, soot stained, brick walls and including the basement, they were three-storeys high. The iron railings at the front were painted in black and had points like spears. The front door of our house was also painted black like the railings outside and it seemed huge in comparison to the front door of our baranga. The door of 189, Southgate Road was like the gate of a fortress that could only be opened by the special key that my father produced from his pocket. Once unlocked and opened, I was surprised that there were no soldiers on guard duty. I had expected some to be there, standing to attention, guarding the gate. My imagination was in full flow.

We entered the house in some suspense, not knowing what to expect. Inside, we stood in a long, wide, dark passage leading to a dark stairway that went both to the upper floor and down into the underground shadows of a basement. The eerie darkness felt spooky and unsettling to me.

"I'm frightened," my sister whispered.

This made me feel even more nervous. Beyond the staircase there was a door that led to the back of the house which was used as a kitchen. Suddenly, my father switched on the passage light.

"Don't be frightened, Fotaki! Don't be frightened, Kika!" he said in a playful tone.

He had noticed our expressions when we were facing the darkness of the basement.

"You have nothing to worry about. Mr Christos and Mrs Chrystalla are the landlords and they are very nice people. They will be your friends. You will meet them in the morning."

I was happy that there was light because my imagination was getting the better of me. I imagined that like Odysseus, I was trapped in the dark cave of Polyphemos. But even with the light on, it still felt quite strange. This huge house with linoleum floor covering and electric lighting, with so many rooms was bewildering. Our baranga had only two rooms and Grandmother's house had no staircase or electric lighting. We had relied on oil lamps to shed some light during the evening hours. Every corner of the passage was now well lit by the magical electric bulb and this quickly dispersed my fears of the dark. I continued to be impressed and my imagination had been stimulated. I was convinced that this was a castle, and to my utter amazement, we were going to live in it. No one was going to capture our castle, we were going to defend it like real knights. Despite being very excited with my new home, there was still the uncertainty about whether we were really going to stay there. Not all my questions had been answered satisfactorily. What about my school in Varosi? What about my friends on the beach? When could I go to the beach? I needed to know.

"Is this where we are going to live, Mama?" I asked repeatedly.

"Is this where we are going to live?"

"Yes, my dear, this is where we are going to live from now on. This is our new home."

"But Mama, when are we going home to Varosi? All my friends are there and I want to play with them. Mama, when will I see my friends again?"

Mother looked at me with a sad expression but made no attempt to answer my questions. My sister answered for her.

"Don't be silly, Fotaki! We are staying here. Do you think we came all this way so that we can just go straight back? We are in England now!"

My sister spoke with a tone of authority that was very new to me and it was as if she was telling me to not bother our mother who was so anxious and tired after our long journey, with questions that had an obvious answer.

Our kind landlords, Christos and his wife Chrystalla had been in England for some years and were more established then the recent arrivals. They proved to be a very welcoming and kind couple. They had cooked some food for us because they knew that we would be hungry. The food was left on the stove in our kitchen. There was a hot 'avgolemoni', egg lemon soup with boiled chicken to eat. The driver ate with us, and after my father had paid him for his trouble, wished us goodnight and left. My sister and I were put to bed in one room.

As I lay there trying to warm up between the cold sheets and blankets, I could hear my parents talking quietly in the next room. Across our dark bedroom, my sister was already fast asleep. I was slumbering between sleep and wakefulness; everything that I had seen on that day of our arrival flashed through my mind: the great railway station with all its movement and noise of people and machines, the lights of the streets, the shops and the innumerable men and women wrapped in their overcoats, briskly walking onwards to their destinations, appeared in the eye of my imagination. How puzzling it was now to find myself in a big, dark room with tall windows and a high ceiling, in a house unlike any that I had been in before, in a city called 'Londino' in a country called 'Anglia', where all the people spoke 'Englezika', a language that I could not understand.

Gradually, with the quiet voices of my parents fading into the night, while they planned and looked forward to a happier and more certain future, I also succumbed to my tiredness and in my sleep, my dream took me back to the beach at Varosi, running on the hot sand with my friends. I saw my grandparents and my aunties at our last farewell with tears in their eyes, waving their hands, calling out goodbye with sad voices. I dreamed of our ship cutting through the waves and the train roaring through dark tunnels and valleys under dark skies and I dreamed of standing in front of a huge closed door with my sister and mother, with our suitcases by our sides, waiting for the door to open.

~

Thousands of Cypriots during the 1950s and 1960s made their way to England. At the beginning, the usual means of the journey was by ship and train. Later, air travel became more accessible and people from Cyprus began travelling to England by air. There were, of course, Cypriots in London who had arrived pre-war. It was the custom amongst them to gather together to exchange news, to give one another support. Thus, if one Cypriot managed to open a business, he employed other Cypriots. In the restaurants, or in the rag trade 'sweatshops', the budding Cypriot businessmen employed their fellow Cypriots; often they were members of the same family or had come from the same village or, perhaps, from the same town. If you asked any of these people why they had come to England, they said that they wanted to work, to build some kind of a future and even in those early days, it was clear to many that to achieve their dream, they needed to be engaged in business and to have their own house. From such simple beginnings, many families, as the years passed, were able to achieve a remarkable prosperity. The dilapidated and decaying structures from the Victorian era, with the pungent, metal dustbins, often overflowing with rubbish, outside of every front door, were not exactly very appealing but to purchase even a house that was decaying and in an area that was unwelcoming and unpleasant was a first step to gaining a foothold, becoming more secure. What did it matter if the houses needed to be virtually gutted and totally refurbished? It could all be done in the long term. The truth is that most Cypriots did not relish the idea of buying and living in those decaying buildings, most of which were infested with all kinds of vermin. But it was a beginning in a new land. And, of course, nobody had, at that time, heard of the amazing London property boom that was about to manifest itself to the delight and joy of property owners in general including the members of the Cypriot community who had bought older properties in London in areas like Islington, Camden, Finsbury Park, whose price, soon after, rocketed beyond the hemisphere. It was an unexpected bonanza; it was the turning of the wheel of fortune and many poor, economic immigrants from Cyprus, who had scraped the small deposit together to get a mortgage from a building society, were in for a very pleasant surprise.

~

My mother and father began with the same dreams and aspirations. They worked extremely hard. Father found work in factories around Dagenham. Unlike many other Cypriots, he never tried or was never inclined to have his own business. It wasn't in his character to be ambitious. He never felt the need to accumulate money or property. It was more important for him to live for the moment. 'Carpe Dium' could very well have been his motto.

Mother worked in the rag trade. She worked normal working hours and often brought work home so that she could earn some extra money in the evenings. After some years, she bought a sewing machine. It was a 'Singer', an industrial, electrical model. She became a home worker. Bundles of pieces of dresses, blouses or other items of clothes were delivered from the factory. When they were sewn into finished garments, they were collected. For each dress, the machinist was paid a few shillings. The machinists worked at home, cleaned, cooked and looked after the children. They supported the endeavours of their husbands. Mortgages were undertaken, businesses were established and thus, the economic life of the community had its very humble beginnings.

The winter of 1957 was severe. It was often freezing at night and in the day, the mixture of fog and soot from thousands of chimneys across London blended to create smog, a toxic mixture that was sometimes lethal to those that breathed it. Children and elderly people and those with asthma or other breathing complications suffered the most. In 1952, more than 12,000 people died as a result of the smog. The Cypriots often joked that in the lack of visibility, you could bump into a lamp post and say sorry. The fog or smog and the freezing cold had an immediate effect on me. We lived in freezing cold rooms with no central heating. I developed a flu and severe cough, my temperature soared. I was ill for about three weeks. It was the impact of coming from a warm Mediterranean climate to a cold, damp and polluted environment. It was the one and only time that I suffered in this manner. I suppose it was a question of acclimatising and this I did very quickly. In the years that followed, I distinctly remember making my way to school through the thick, sulphurous fog, hardly being able to see three feet in front of me. At school, my friends and I would take our white handkerchiefs and exhale hard onto them. When we checked the result of our experiment, we saw how our white handkerchiefs became speckled with the soot and grime that we had breathed into them. The awful pollution was not only inhaled in the streets but sometimes it invaded the interior of buildings. Houses and hospitals, schools and factories, offices, pubs and bars were all invaded by the sulphurous substance that found its way into every nook and cranny of the city. No place escaped, no person was left unaffected by it.

Terrible as it might have been, the city covered by a blanket of fog inspired my imagination. Was this the underworld covered in mists and smoke where the ghosts of the dead resided? Is this where Odysseus came to speak with the ghost of Teresias[1] to seek directions for his way home? Like Odysseus, I wondered in the haze of the fog, thinking that I would encounter the ghost of a fallen warrior from Troy. The only people that I ever met, however, were my mates on the way to school.

1. Lines 112-152, Book XI, *The Odyssey*, Homer. Translated by Robert Fitzgerald. Everyman.

Part 3: An Evolvement

Lego

Before long, my mother, with the help of our landlady who could communicate fairly clearly in English, took me to the local primary school. It was De Beauvoir Infants & Juniors School in Balls Pond Road, Dalston. This was just off Southgate Road where we lived. A little before my birthday, I found myself in an English school and not understanding a word that was spoken to me. I suppose in a child's manner; I was very impressed with this school. It was an old Victorian building with little concrete staircases for the children leading onto a big hall with shiny parquet flooring that smelled of polish. The walls in the hall and corridors were covered in large framed prints of famous paintings. There were large displays of the children's work: pictures done in paint or in crayons of many colours. Some displays showed the use of numbers while others contained children's hand writing. The large busy classrooms were around this hall. I was very excited and I didn't need to understand the language to see that in my new classroom, there were paints, sugar paper of every colour, colouring pencils, scissors and Lego, something entirely new to me. There were toys and books full of bright, attractive pictures. The children were reading and writing, drawing and painting, cutting and sticking colour paper into patterns. Every child was busy with their own activity, engaged in the process of learning, engrossed with imaginative creativity.

I looked on in wonder; I had never seen anything like it before. I loved it, particularly because I could feel that the children and the adults appeared very friendly, friendly and warm towards me. I was encouraged to join in, to paint and draw, to build Lego, to write the letters of the alphabet. It was with great pride that at the end of my first day at a London school, I took home a picture that I had painted. It was supposed to be a sailing ship with a big square sail. The sea was a deep blue and the sun was bright yellow. At the centre of my sailing ship, I added the figure of a sailor. It represented King Odysseus, triumphant, strong, heroic, sailing on to new adventures.

The next day, I couldn't wait to go back to school. My excitement was enormous. I had lost old friends with whom I roamed on the sandy beach of Varosi but now I was delighted that I had made new friends and that I was going to a school that was full of interesting things to do. On the second day of my new school, I began to speak some simple words of the language that I would learn quickly and eventually study and love.

"Ya wanna play football?" asked my new friend.

He was a little boy with fair, straight hair and bright blue eyes. He looked at me, smiled and held the ball up.

"Football," I said, by which I meant 'yes'.

So, we both ran down the narrow staircase, jumping down the small steps designed by some intelligent, Victorian architect, for the convenience of infants and juniors, then out on to the playground. We kicked the ball around, shouted and enjoyed ourselves as only little boys could. Within a minute or two, other little boys joined in our game. I played with them, kicking and passing the ball, making runs towards the goal mouth, calling for the ball and trying to impress my new mates with my football skills. It was as if I had always been with them, a friend from the beginning. How wonderful! I felt welcomed and befriended. My shyness and uncertainty had left me. I felt happy; I had a sense of belonging. I was not a strange little boy from far away, who spoke a strange language that nobody understood. This was my new school; it was clean and tidy, full of books and toys, where all the children wanted to be my friends and where the teachers smiled at me in a warm and kindly manner.

I had settled into my new school very quickly. My parents were both working, and my sister began to attend the local secondary school. We were in London and we had now begun the process of settling into our new lives. In fact, Cyprus and my old friends, the sandy beach at Varosi, were now in the background…but not forgotten. My grandmother and the village seemed geographically distant but emotionally close. The people who had been a part of our lives remained in our minds and sometimes we referred to them as if they lived just around the corner and would appear at any time for a quick chat. We constantly spoke about my grandparents, my uncles and aunties, about Sotira, Styloi and Varosi. These were important subjects in our thoughts and our conversations. Our old world was very much with us; it was real and tangible and would only begin to fade away with the passing of generations.

While remembering our previous life in Cyprus with fondness and love, we instinctively understood that we had to embrace the present and face the challenges that lay ahead.

I was captivated and entranced by my new world and particularly by my new school. Of all the schools in the whole wide world, my new school was for me the best. In my excitement and enthusiasm, this is how I really felt. Creative activity had sparked the desire to learn. I drew patterns and coloured them in. I wrote the letters of the English alphabet and spoke some words like 'thank you', 'please', 'excuse me, Miss', 'May I have…' and so on. However, not everything turned out to be as pleasant or as smooth as my initial experiences and I was soon to discover that in our brave new world, there could also be hurtful and damaging events and where there were undercurrents of feelings and emotions that I did not understand and from which I needed protection:

One day in class, I was playing with some Lego. I had a box of white coloured Lego and I was busy constructing a castle. While I was silently, studiously and seriously engaged in this activity, lost in the imaginary world of play, another little boy came and tried to take my box of Lego away from me. I was beginning to feel less shy, competitive and more confident in my new environment. So I resisted.

"No! No!" I exclaimed. 'No' was one of the few words that I had learnt.

While this was going on, I had noticed that the teacher, who was an elderly lady in spectacles, was looking at what was going on from the other side of the room. She stood still with her hands on her hips and stared at the scuffle that had developed between the other boy and me. I was desperately holding on to my Lego while the other boy was trying to wrench the box from my grip. It was the kind of thing that children sometimes do and all that is required is for a responsible adult to sooth the situation with a few words about the importance of sharing.

"Let me have it! Let me have it!" the other little boy screamed.

"No! No! No!" I repeated over and over again.

The teacher held off for a few moments more while the tussle and shouting continued. Pieces of Lego spilled onto the floor. I could see the angry expression on the elderly teacher's face. Her eyes were glaring as she began to move slowly and purposefully towards us. I had thought that she was going to stop the other little boy from taking the Lego from me. I wanted to complain that I had been playing with the Lego first, but my English was not yet sufficient to say this.

When she had approached us, she firmly took my hand and allowed the other boy to keep the Lego that I had been playing with. I had stopped struggling and looked up at her stern grey eyes and firm thin lips. I was surprised. I was even more surprised when she then roughly rolled up my sleeve and smacked me four or five times, very hard, on the bare arm.

"That will teach you to fight with other people for things that don't belong to you! Let that be a lesson to you!"

Her face was very red and her voice was full of anger. The smack on the arm had stung me but worse than that was my confusion. I was very bewildered. I was confused. I was emotionally hurt. I didn't know what to do. I had expected her to allow me to keep the Lego and to take the other boy away. I had expected protection and justice but instead, I was smacked, shouted at, shocked and shaken. I felt a deep humiliation. There was silence in the class as the other children stared speechless at me and at the angry teacher. Everything came to a sudden halt, activity ceased, there was silence and tension. The violence inflicted upon me had surprised them. Never before had they seen their kind teacher behave in such a way towards a child in her class. The teacher then just walked away without saying anything else and carried on as if nothing had happened. I was left standing in the middle of the classroom, not understanding anyone, not knowing what to do and feeling the intense shame of a little child that had been wronged and whose self-esteem had been shattered.

I didn't cry and I didn't move. I remained standing in the middle of the room, looking down at some scattered Lego around my feet. Though in my childish mind, I did not have an understanding of the meaning of justice, I was, nevertheless, overwhelmed with the feeling of having been wronged. I had been treated unfairly, unjustly, in an unwarranted manner. I felt hot, embarrassed and degraded. Somehow, I held back my tears. After perhaps a minute or so, but which seemed like an hour, a young assistant teacher approached me and spoke softly.

"Come on, let's go and do some painting."

She indicated that I should follow her. She took me by the hand. Her voice was gentle and reassuring. I followed her to a table where she gave me some paints and brushes. I picked up the brush and dipped it into a jar of water and then onto the dry water colour paint. I painted in silence and not wanting to look up at anyone. I felt the corners of my mouth turning down, my chin quivering, my face was hot, but somehow, I continued to hold back the tears as I carried on painting my picture. When I had finished, I stood slightly back and examined it with care. It showed a little white house with a green door. The sky above was a deep blue and was cloudless. The sun was a bright yellow with thick rays that extended to the ground. In front of the little house, there was the figure of what appeared to be a woman with a long, black dress and a black kerchief around her face. Next to her, stood a man with a long, black moustache, wearing a *vraka*, the traditional Cyprus baggy trousers and holding a *matsuka*, a long shepherd's staff. They both had smiling faces. I felt as if they were smiling at me. As I looked at this simple picture, I began to have a child's understanding of the meaning and value of the life that we had left behind. I also realised with the same child's understanding that this new world, that had initially appeared to be so wonderful, could also be unpredictable, unpleasant and unwelcoming; more than that, the smiling faces of the figures in painting made me feel that I should be strong and not be defeated.

When Mother arrived home that evening, she asked me in her usual manner what I had been doing at school and whether I had enjoyed my day.

"Did you have a nice day at school? Have you learnt some more new words in English? Come on, Fotaki, let me hear you talk some of this new language!"

She had developed the habit of trying to coax me into saying something in the new language that I was learning and remembering her lack of schooling, she felt proud that I was attending what she thought was such a good school with very caring teachers.

"I want to learn some English as well. Teach me what you learnt today, Fotaki, please," she implored.

"Today I learnt how to say 'smack' but I don't know what it means. The other children were saying this word to me."

"Smack? Tomorrow you ought to ask your teacher the meaning of this word. She will explain the meaning, I am sure. What else did you do?"

"I played with some toys and something called Lego but best of all I painted a picture of Grandmother and Grandfather."

My words brought a proud smile to her face.

"One day you will go to a great English university and become a gifted artist, then, you will paint beautiful pictures and earn a lot of money."

The smile on Mother's face instinctively made me feel that I had been smacked by the very person that she had felt was kind and protective. My instinct told me that if she had known this, it would have made her feel terribly unhappy and so I smiled at Mother and didn't say a word.

Strangers in a Foreign Land

In 1957, the EOKA struggle for union with Greece was entering a bitter phase. EOKA fighters engaged the British forces on the island. British soldiers and interests became targets and often innocent people suffered both among the Cypriots and amongst the British. Feelings in Cyprus had reached fever pitch. The Cypriots felt betrayed by the British for whom they had fought in both world wars. The Greek nation had always been a constant ally of Britain. The Cypriots could not understand how the British now refused to grant an island which was predominantly Greek in every respect and had shown such loyalty to Britain, the right to its political aspirations to unite with 'Mother Greece'. There was encouragement in the past from the British that one day Cyprus would be granted this right. The offer had previously been made but was not taken up.[1] During the Second World War, Prime Minister Winston Churchill was impressed by the heroic 'Oxi' of General Metaxa, the Greek leader, given in response to the Italian ultimatum to surrender. This was followed by the remarkable Greek campaign in Albania during which Italian forces were defeated and pushed back. Churchill then hinted that the Cypriots would find fulfilment in their political aspirations for union with Greece but after the war, when the issue of Cyprus was debated in the House of Commons, the aspirations of the Cypriots were ridiculed. In the cruel light of day, Britain's position was that it could never relinquish control of this strategically invaluable island[2]; this was particularly so after Britain's humiliation in Egypt and loss of control of the Suez Canal in 1956. An amusing anecdote to these events is when Winston Churchill is said to have refused to have Cypriot currents as a part of the ingredients for his birthday cake. He was angry with the Cypriots for daring to challenge British rule over the island.

Colonel George Grivas was the military leader of the EOKA campaign. The EOKA group numbered perhaps a few hundred combatants. They were well organised, daring and believed in the justice of their cause. They managed to tie down 30,000 British soldiers. Archbishop Makarios III was the political leader of EOKA and had become an internationally recognised figure, some would say of equal importance to Jomo Kanyata, leader of the Mau Mau and first President of Kenya, Dr Milton Nkruma of Ghana and perhaps a grander comparison with Mahatma Ghandi of India. EOKA claimed that its cause was that of freedom and liberty against colonial oppression. But despite the independence of India and the humiliating withdrawal from Egypt, the British Government had not yet come to a full understanding that the decline of the Empire was spiralling out of control. It wanted to confront the independence movements in Africa and Asia. It failed.

Cyprus, however, was a very small country with less than half a million people. It was easier to deal with. The great British Empire was now like a toothless lion and with its last gasp, was determined to hold on to at least this last remaining corner of its possessions and so attitudes became polarised. The Cypriots could not see the harsh realities of world politics that Cyprus was militarily of great value to British and western interest and that it had to be controlled and so they demanded Enosis (union with Greece) with almost total disregard for the political position of the Turkish Cypriot minority and how the British might use the Turkish Cypriots to dent the aspirations for Enosis of the Greek Cypriots. The British Government could not understand how this small nation of about half a million people could have the audacity to make such a demand from them…so on the day when the EOKA gunman Nikos Sampson[3], who had been accused of the murder of Sergeant Carter and Sergeant Thorogood, two police officers stationed in Cyprus, was acquitted, the British press reported the story in an inflammatory manner with reference to Ledra Street as being 'Murder Mile' and implying that Cypriots were cold-blooded murderers. The usually cool, patient and moderate British public became incensed, intolerant and violently indiscriminate as a result of the news reports. The explosive headlines had succeeded in their provocation which, in turn, resulted in teddy boy attacks against innocent Cypriots on the streets of London.

It is possible that the elderly teacher who had probably read the news story on her way to work, of how the callous Cypriot murderer of Sergeant Carter and Sergeant Thorogood had escaped justice, felt a great indignation at such a miscarriage of justice and perhaps, unthinkingly vented her anger on the little innocent Cypriot boy in her care who for historical and economic reasons had found himself in her classroom on that morning.

In the evening of that very same day, Father was due to return home from work at his usual time. Mother had prepared the evening meal and we had been waiting for the sound of the front door and for his familiar footsteps on the creaking stairs. He was a little late and it was not with his usual smile that he entered. We were shocked to see that he had been badly

119

beaten about the face. His face was bruised and covered in blood; his eyes were black and swollen. As he staggered into the room, my mother let out a cry,

"My God, what has happened to you?"

She rushed to him and helped him to a chair. He tried to calm my mother down.

"I am not really hurt badly. I will be alright. Just clean the blood off my face with some hot water with a little salt in it."

He bravely smiled at my sister and me, but his voice trembled and I could sense that he was quite shaken by his awful experience. As Mother began to clean his wounds, he gave us an account of what had befallen him:

"It was after work. I was just standing quietly at the bus stop, near the end of the queue. There was no sign of the bus, so we were all waiting. There were a few men there from the factory, but I did not know them. Suddenly, three men appeared. They were young, perhaps twenty-five years old or so. They pushed in front of me, but I did not say anything to them because I knew that there would be trouble. But all the time, they were looking at me, staring hard into my eyes. Then one of them suddenly shouted, 'Why are you looking at me, you f***ing Greek bastard!' and at the same time, all three of them attacked me, kicking and punching me to the ground. There was no one to help me. The other people at the bus stop moved out of the way, not wanting to get involved, perhaps they were frightened; who knows why they stood to one side and allowed a fellow human being to be treated in such a way? After a few minutes, the thugs ran off laughing and jeering."

He stopped talking for a moment and as we looked on, we knew that he was not physically hurt badly but his dignity as a person had been dealt a blow. My mother was perplexed and frightened and because at that time, there was no one to help or to reassure us, my parents felt isolated and unwanted, unwanted in a land that was strange to us and was now becoming hostile.

"It was a mistake to come here," she said.

"We have put ourselves in great danger. In Cyprus, we were poor but at least no one attacked us in the streets. Our children have become targets. What are we supposed to do, sit here until something terrible happens to us?"

Even though it was Father who had suffered the attack, he was on this occasion calmer and patient. It was Mother who was panicking and full of apprehensions about our safety.

"Andriana," he said. "I know that this is a terrible thing that has happened, but it will pass. The people who attacked me were just thugs.

There are many good people here who want to be friends and who want to help. We are not going to run away with the first difficulty that we have."

"What about our children when they are going and coming from school? Are you certain that they will be safe, or will we come home one day to find that they have been attacked and beaten by these cruel people, like the ones who have attacked you today?"

By now, Mother's emotions had overwhelmed her and tears began to flow from her eyes and her face that was filled with an intense, troubled expression of sadness. My father stood up, he gently put her in his arms in a reassuring manner.

"They would not dare touch children. The law is very strong here. Such a thing would not be permitted to happen. This little gang who attacked me are not important people. They are nothing more than thugs! The law will catch up with them. This is just a little set back; it doesn't mean that we have to give up on everything and run away!"

Mother's shock and anger could not be soothed so easily. The fear she had for our safety was intense and real. She was gripped by a sense of insecurity, fear and impending disaster.

"Tell me," she shouted at my father with fury and disbelief, thinking that he was both stupid and naive, "what will we do when these thugs all gather together into a great horde and attack our homes or when we are walking in the street?"

"Such a thing could not happen here!" Father already knew what she was about to say.

"It happened in Constantinople just a couple of years ago. Gangs attacked innocent Greek people in the streets and in their homes and nobody did anything about it. Hundreds of people were murdered because of the troubles in Cyprus. What are we doing here? Let us go home before something terrible happens to us and our children!"

Mother was so emotional that she did not stop to think that Cyprus was also now not a safe place to live and worse, much worse was to follow in Cyprus.

Mother's tears flowed from her eyes. Her cheeks were wet and flushed. She was not convinced by Father's brave words. She continued to blame him for putting us all in danger by coming to a place where we were despised and looked down upon. His defiant words didn't mean anything to her and she kept repeating that we were no longer safe. Her fear was turning into a panic.

"We are in danger!" she kept repeating. "They will harm the children! We are in danger! We are not safe here! These people don't want us here. We should go back to Cyprus, at least there, nobody bothered us."

She was shaking with anger and angst. She was fearful, frightened of what the future could unfold.

"Calm down," my father implored. "You will upset the children even more. It has been a very bad day and we will get over it, now please, stop crying."

Just then, the electricity switched off and we were immersed in darkness. Father was flat broke and did not even have any pennies to put into the electricity metre to give us at least the comfort of some light. The only thing left to do was to go to bed. We felt wretched, unloved, unwanted, and unwelcomed, cold and without light. Through that night, I could hear my mother gently and quietly weeping, trying to the best of her ability to muffle the sounds of her sorrow so that my sister and I would not be disturbed even more than we had been already. Even so, we could still hear her.

"What will become of us… What will become of us in this place…? I want to go home, I want to go home, my children are in danger… Where is my mother and father who were always close to us, who always helped and protected us…"

She cried miserably in the darkness of the night. My father did not reply.

The traumatic events of that day had made us feel like unwanted intruders, strangers in a foreign land who were looked upon with hostility and suspicion. It was from then on that I began to have a sense of my otherness, that I was not entirely like other children and that I did not belong. I had been smacked at school by my teacher for a reason that I did not understand. My father had been attacked on the street on his way home from work. My mother had shed tears of fear and anxiety because she worried that my sister and I would come to some harm on the way home from school. How could we and other people like us, with similar experiences, not feel persecuted and unwanted? It was a moment of crises and we felt alienated with our environment. Father had calculated that wherever you may go, if you are honest, hardworking and make a contribution to society, you would be accepted, you would be given respect and the rights of a citizen. He was right in thinking these things but on that day, when I had been smacked by my teacher, on that evening, when Father had been attacked by racist thugs at a bus stop on his way home from work, we all felt that England was full of dangerous thugs who were determined to persecute us. The moment of crises past and we realised that the experience of that awful day was not going to be typical. It was the exception. In due course, we were to discover the wisdom of Father's words. There were some unpleasant incidents, but these were far outweighed by the experiences of general kindness, consideration and care that we encountered amongst the people in whose country we had decided to come and live in. Many people were genuinely friendly, fair and helpful.

1. Cyprus was offered by the British to Greece in 1915. In exchange, Britain wanted Greece to join the war and in particular to help support Serbia. Greek-Cypriot Enosis of October 1915. *A Lost Opportunity?* Balkan Studies, Stavros Terry Stavridis. Page 289.

2. During the debates in the House of Commons relating to the Cyprus Question, 1954–1955, the high ranking British diplomat, Henry Hopkinson stated: "It has always been understood and agreed that there are certain territories in the Commonwealth which owing to particular circumstances, can never expect to be fully independent." Great Power Politics. Achilles C. Emilianidis. Cambridge Scholars.

3. Nicos Sampson, the 'executioner of Murder Mile' who two times escaped the British death sentence. The Guardian, Obituary, Kosta Pavlowich, 21st May, 2001.

Guy Fawkes

A few days before the 5th of November, I decided that I was going to make a 'Guy' and collect some money to buy fireworks. I must have been eight or nine years old. The gun powder plot was celebrated in a big way in England and junior schools focused on this festival. The children studied the history of the Stuarts and drew pictures of Guido De Fawkes surrounded by kegs of gunpowder. My class room was transformed into a hive of activity. Some children painted a fireworks display with a splash of red, orange, yellow and white colours. Other groups of children were drawing and colouring in the portrait of the great conspirator who had plotted to blow up the Houses of Parliament or they wrote stories or were reading about how the plot was discovered in the nick of time and the Parliament was saved from the Catholics, the terrorists of that time.

The story of the Catholic conspiracy interested me. In class, I drew my own picture of Guido De Fawkes. It showed him wearing a huge, high, black hat. I drew him with a black pointed beard and prominent black eye brows. When I had finished the picture, I felt very proud of myself. Drawing and colouring was one area in which I was as good as the other children because it did not require the use of the English language with which I was still only a beginner. Despite this, I was eager for my teacher's approval because I wanted to feel as good and as able as the other children who were constantly receiving praise and rewards. I had seen how the teacher smiled and spoke encouraging words whenever a boy or girl held up their drawings and writing for his approval.

"Well done, Susan, that's a really good picture of Guy Fawkes. You can have a gold star for that!"

He moved on to another pupil.

"Tom, that is a lot of writing that you have done and it is so neat. I like that, Tom, you're really doing your best. You can have a star as well and keep up the good work!"

He smiled kindly at the members of his class while constantly giving them encouragement and praise.

I noticed how the little girl named Susan beamed with pride and smiled with happiness because of the teacher's kind words and the shiny gold star sticker that he had awarded her. The teacher walked around the class, praising and rewarding the children. I expected him to also come to me, but he did not. Eventually, he went and sat behind his desk from where he observed us working on our drawings and writing in our books. He had not come to me. I thought that he had missed me out by accident. I had seen how kind he had been to all the children. Yes, he was a very kind man and all I had to do was to walk over to his desk and present him with my work. He was a very kind man who was going to smile at me and stick a gold star on my work like he did for other children… I then took my drawing of Guido De Fawkes and ceremoniously presented it to my teacher who was still sitting at his desk at the front of the class. He took one look at my picture, stood up to attract the attention of the class and with an artificial laugh exclaimed in a loud voice,

"Why, he looks like that terrorist fellow from your country…you know that Archbishop Makarios or whatever his name is, who is always trying to blow up our soldiers. He is just like him."

I understood the word Makarios because he had pronounced it so loudly and also because my parents and their friends often mentioned this name in their discussions, but I could not make out the meaning of what he was saying to the class. The other children were surprised by the tone of his voice. They thought that their teacher wanted to share a joke with them and they were eager to respond. Through some intuition, I felt the teacher's hostility and even though the other children were giggling, I did not join in the laughter. I was confused by my teacher's reaction. I had expected some praise. He had always been a very kind man who sometimes smiled at me in an encouraging way. I was not sure why he now spoke in such a manner and why everyone was laughing at my picture. I stood at the front of the class, looking from my teacher's grimace to the laughing faces of the other boys and girls. I couldn't understand why they were laughing, I was confused, I was bewildered, I was trying to understand. Should I have joined in the laughter? What were they laughing at? What was the joke? Were they laughing at me? The teacher's face had become like a malevolent mask wearing a hostile grin. My fellow pupils, who a few minutes earlier were serene, sensible and softly spoken had become a gang arrayed against me. They were screaming and shouting and their mocking faces were all turned towards me. They were laughing in an uncontrollable manner as if they could not believe that their noise was not being challenged by the teacher. They were like prisoners who had been constrained for a long time, who now had a brief moment of freedom and were desperate to make the most it. They continued to laugh and jeer at me, they were yelling words that I could not comprehend.

"Terrorist!"
"Foreigner!"
"Terrorist!"

I stood in silence, surprised at the sudden change in the attitude of my teacher and of my fellow pupils, who a short while before were being pleasant and kind towards me. I felt yet again, humiliated in the classroom. I was a spectacle while all around me was a mob with unfriendly faces. The teacher then handed me my exercise book and indicated with a motion of his head that I should sit down. I took my book and with downcast eyes, I walked slowly back to my desk. I sat rigidly without looking at any one.

Gradually, all the noise ceased and the class resumed its normal activity without anyone paying further heed to me. I looked down at my drawing of Guido De Fawkes with the kegs of gunpowder stacked up all around him and with a lit torch in his hands. What did my teacher mean when he said that my picture looked like that 'Makarios fellow'? I was made to feel that I had done something quite bad and so, I took up my pencil and drew lines across my drawing until it had been totally defaced.

Looking back on this incident, I can only conjecture that my drawing reminded the teacher of Archbishop Makarios because of my Greek Cypriot ethnicity and that his anger was aroused because Makarios, just like Guido De Fawkes, was responsible for acting against The Crown. The politics of Cyprus and the EOKA campaign against the British had aroused emotions. My kind teacher's emotions had been provoked; he was angry because British soldiers were being shot at in Cyprus. Unfortunately, he associated a child in his class with those who he believed were to blame for the crises in Cyprus and wanted to punish me. On that afternoon, in my primary school in Dalston, I had become the scapegoat and for a brief moment, I had been victimised, cast out, ostracised, blamed for the cruel events that were unfolding in a political crisis in my now former and distant homeland. Blood had been shed there, the feelings of primitive tribalism had been evoked so that even a teacher in a London school, for a moment or two thought and behaved without ethical judgement. I felt alone, separated from those around me. I didn't understand my teacher's motives or why my fellow pupils jeered at that time, but I remember feeling very upset because I had not been praised for my endeavours or awarded a gold star for my work.

Fireworks

I must have been a resilient little chap because I soon pushed this unpleasant experience to the back of my mind. I was determined that like other children, I was going to celebrate Guy Fawkes Day and nothing was going to deter me.

One of the first rhymes that I learnt in the English language was the chant of Guy Fawkes:

"Please do remember

The 5th of November,

Gun powder, treason and plot!"

My friends at school had already collected masses of fireworks for the occasion. Some of my friends brought them to school, hidden in their bags to show the rest of us what they had collected. I had never seen fireworks before, so I was very excited and I desperately wanted to buy some to join in the celebration. I looked at fireworks on sale in shop windows. I had learnt the names of the different varieties. There were bangers and Spinning Catherine Wheels, crackerjacks and sparklers but best of all were the rockets. They came in a variety of sizes, ranging from the very small to the very large and expensive. I looked on but in the back of my mind, I remembered how my parents had said that we had no money for fireworks, they cost too much and that I was not to go on the streets and beg for money for the purpose of buying fireworks.

"Fotaki," my mother said, "I don't want you to go anywhere while we are at work. I have seen those boys begging for money on the streets. Don't dare to do such a thing because I will be very angry with you."

"Mama, the English boys are not begging," I argued. "They are collecting money for the great festival of Guy Fawkes. They will buy fireworks with the money and they will have a great time. Why can't I do that?"

I wanted to persuade her by showing how much I had learnt about this subject.

"My teacher said that Guy Fawkes was a great Catholic terrorist who fought against the King. He was just like Makarios my teacher said. He put gun powder in the cellars of the Houses of Parliament but he was

127

captured before he could light the fuse and they executed him by cutting off his head. My teacher said that Makarios should also be executed because he tries to kill British soldiers but he should be hanged instead of having his head cut off."

My mother looked astonished at what I was saying.

"I have told you, Fotaki," she now warned in a firm voice, "if you dare to go on the street and ask for money like a beggar and I find out that you have disobeyed my instructions, you will be in serious trouble. Do you understand?"

"Yes, Mama, I understand what you are saying," I answered with reluctance but without much conviction.

"And there is something else I want you to try and understand," she continued in a very serious manner.

"Makarios is not like the person you have described; he is not a terrorist. He is the Archbishop of Cyprus, he is very intelligent and he is fighting for the freedom of our country."

I didn't quite understand what she was talking about, but I looked at her earnestly in the eyes and nodded as if I had fully comprehended her meaning and that I was in absolute agreement with her.

I had been given a stern warning by my mother regarding this matter, but it was of no avail. I knew that Mother could be very strict with me if she was disobeyed about something important, but I felt desperate to have the fireworks. I was reckless and determined to do what I had planned. So, one morning, when they went off to work and my sister at that time was working in the same clothes factory as my mother, I got out of bed, quickly dressed and then began to construct a very odd-looking Guy. I found an old pair of trousers and an old pullover. I tied the ends of the sleeves of the pullover and of the trouser legs with a piece of string and stuffed them with newspapers rolled up into balls. I crudely tied the torso and the legs together and then constructed a head with more rolled up paper upon which I stuck a circular piece of cardboard with a smiling face drawn upon it. I then stepped back and looked at my construction. It must have been the most unconvincing model of a Guy in all the history of Guy making and I felt its limitations, but I was determined to see my forbidden adventure through to its conclusion.

At that time, we were living in Islington Green, before it had become 'yuppified'. Our house was situated in the connecting road facing Islington Green Park, linking Essex Road with Upper Street. On the far side, going towards the Angel, stood the statue of Sir Hugh Myddleton, an Elizabethan engineer, and on the opposite side, next door to our house, was the old but once famous Collins Music Hall which by then had been closed due to a fire. I took the odd-looking Guy that I had constructed and

128

placed him in a sitting position on the pavement, outside The King's Head, a pub across the road from the Rex Cinema.

It was fairly early in the morning and it was somewhat cold with a fresh wind. Most people who walked by just looked straight ahead, ignoring me, perhaps they were thinking of their work day and what was ahead of them. Some people smiled but hurried on and sometimes they smiled broadly and dropped a copper coin into the small box in front of my Guy. If my parents had seen me, I'm certain that they would have been angry and disappointed by my thoughtless disobedience.

It wasn't long before I had begun to accumulate a fair number of pennies and I was getting excited at the prospect of going to the local shop to buy some really good fireworks. I had seen a box on display with an assortment of fireworks in it. On the lid of the box, there was a picture of Guy Fawkes with a little pointed beard, wearing a tall hat and carrying a lantern in his hand. It was just like the picture that I had drawn at school. This was the box of fireworks that I wanted. I wanted it more than anything else. All my friends at school would be getting masses of fireworks so why shouldn't I at least have a few. It was only fair, and I was keen to make my purchase as soon as possible. I needed five shillings and six pence in total but I did not as yet have this amount and so, I stood there in the cold, looking for the next passer-by who might provide an addition to my funds. Just then, from the corner of my eye, I caught a glimpse of an unusual-looking old man. He walked slowly in my direction, slightly bowed with his arms swinging by his sides which for some strange reason, reminded me of an ape. When he was fairly close, I felt that he was looking piercingly at me. He was quite stout and well dressed in a smart suit. He wore a bowler hat which even at that time was quite rare and carried an umbrella that he used as a walking stick. He was neat, tidy and very red in the face. He kept his eyes on me, but his face remained expressionless. I didn't know how to react. I felt uncertain whether I should venture to ask for a penny or perhaps look the other way and let him pass. When he was just a few feet from me, he looked at my Guy and sneered. I mistook this sign and thought it was some kind of a smile and so I briskly walked up to him like a playful terrier, full of confidence. I looked up and said,

"Penny for the Guy, mister?"

His reaction was cataclysmic.

"So, you want a penny for the Guy, do you? You f***ing Greek bastard! Why don't you sod off back to where you come from!"

For a moment, he stood staring down at me. His face was contorted; his left hand was clenched into a tight fist while in his other hand, he had raised his umbrella like a club. I froze with fear. I stood still, silent, motionless, as if my fear of this angry old man had immobilised me, as if I had been rooted to the spot where I had been standing, as if I was petrified at the sight of this new Medusa. Suddenly, slyly, he looked right and left to check if anyone had been observing his threatening behaviour towards me. Without any further ado, he slunk off in the direction of the Angel, muttering something or other to himself.

The teacher in the classroom had mocked and humiliated me. The old man with the bowler hat had sworn and physically threatened me. These were emotionally hurtful experiences. You really felt pain. There was bewilderment, confusion and questions. Why the hostility? Why such hatred? Why such a lack of empathy? Even at a young age I knew that it was because I was from another land and another culture. It was as if my olive skin and black hair were emblematic and that I was the enemy of the fair, blue-eyed Anglo Saxons. For certain, I was made to feel different from my friends at school; that there was something wrong with me. Perhaps, I couldn't put this feeling into words at that time. It took some years before I could think about the meaning of prejudice or racism and to be able to articulate my thoughts on these disturbing subjects but even as a little boy, I tried in my own way to make sense of the hostility that I sometimes faced in school or on the streets. When I looked in to the mirror, I saw a boy with black hair, dark brown eyes and an olive complexion looking back at me. I looked different from the children with whom I went to school. They were often blonde with blue eyes and fair skin. The difference was sometimes emphasised by other people. Sometimes children at school called me names:

"Bubble and squeak, Greek!"

There were other racist taunts or jokes; sometimes there were hostile looks or comments like,

"Go back to your own country, you bloody foreigner."

"Go home, you, wog!"

Such occurrences happened anywhere: in the streets, on the bus, on the tube, at the shops or market place. It would leave the target of such verbal abuse feeling shocked, isolated, demeaned and angry. There was a kind of crisis between some members of the host community and the recent arrivals from India and Pakistan, from the Caribbean, Cyprus or Africa. Some British people found it impossible to accept the immigrants who had come to live amongst them as fellow human beings and as fellow citizens. There wasn't anything that anyone could say that would change this point of view. On the street level, there was verbal abuse directed at the immigrants. From a pragmatic point of view, housing became a problem particularly for black people. Rooms were advertised for letting on shop notice boards but often a footnote was added on these notices, indicating that 'coloured people' need not apply. Employment was also very problematic for immigrants who irrespective of qualifications, skills or abilities, were often given the most menial jobs. It took years before this sort of prejudice was eliminated. Indeed, a minority of English people seemed to suffer from some kind of genetic condition that prevented them from ridding themselves of the prejudice that they had towards people different from themselves.

However, the good shown by most people in Britain far outweighed the hostility shown by a minority of racists. Anti-racist laws were passed. The Race Relations Act became law in 1965 and it was amended in subsequent years, each time giving further support to those people on the receiving end of racial prejudice. No longer could people from what became the ethnic minorities, have the rights of the ordinary citizen denied to them. Multiculturalism was introduced in schools with the aim of educating children to respect, to learn from and to enjoy each other's cultural heritage.

With political decisions that attempted to integrate the ethnic minority people into the fabric of British society, it must be said that the major political parties had introduced policies and governments had passed laws that reflected a civilised and commendable attitude towards the people who had recently arrived at these shores. This progress was indeed important but just as relevant was the attitude of the many ordinary British people who went out of their way to show that they were friendly and fair towards the new people who had come to live in Britain.

~

Christmas 1957

The winter of 1957 was severe. It was our first experience of the icy cold winds of northern Europe, blowing in from the Arctic. The cold was uncomfortable, unpleasant and unremitting. The snow and ice was like an attacking army that had descended upon the city, forcing the scurrying citizens to seek shelter. Everywhere, there was a hard frost; it pasted on to the pavement the few remaining leaves that had not been swept away by the autumn winds and every day, a freezing fog covered the city like a grey blanket, making everything seem ghostly and cheerless. People went about their business, wrapped up in their over coats; they walked with hunched shoulders as if to protect themselves from the biting wind. The weather for the whole of December was down to freezing point almost every day but on the 17th of December, it fell to -6 centigrade. It was enough to upset the hardiest of souls.

It was particularly difficult for Mother and Father because they had to be up for work as early as 5 o'clock in the morning. This was before central heating could be afforded by most people. The main means of keeping warm was by lighting coal fires but often it was not enough and could hardly take the edge off the cold.

My chief responsibility when I awoke was to light the fire because at that time in the morning, the house was like a giant freezer; the inside of the house wasn't any warmer than the outside temperature, so we desperately needed some warmth. I'd climb out of bed and while still in my pyjamas, I would begin the process of lighting the fire. I started by sweeping the grate clean from the ashes of the previous fire. This created a lot of dust that made me cough quite severely. My sister Kika, who was still in bed, moaned at me.

"Be quiet! You are going to wake up the people upstairs! Don't cough so loudly!"

After breathing in the dust from the grate, I really didn't have much choice, so I continued to cough despite my sister's annoyance with me. When the grate had been cleaned, I proceeded to roll up single sheets of newspapers into small balls and place them into it, like apples in a fruit bowl. Then I took some small sticks that had been already split from a log of wood and I placed them like the struts of a tent over the balls of newspaper. On top of the sticks of wood, I put some large chunks of coal that were kept in a bucket in the corner of the room. Finally, I lit a match and carefully set it to newspaper that could be seen through a gap between the coal and sticks. The newspaper caught fire and in turn, the sticks and coal were also soon alight. My enjoyment of the process and the satisfaction that I had from doing this little job made me feel not only a useful person but gave me joy despite the cold that I felt first thing in the morning.

During this freezing spell, Mother and Father often referred to the wonderful winter sunshine of Cyprus, where you could get through even December and January without even having to put on a jacket, but they never complained because they understood that you cannot live by just having pleasant weather. You also needed to work. How brave they were! How enduring! No matter how cold or wet it might have been, they went to work, they were relentless, never taking a day off, even when they had a bad cold or a cough, when most people would have stayed in bed to recover from their ailment. They were out of the house and off to work before my sister and I were awake. We were left responsible for ourselves. We had to get up, wash, dress, eat something and then walk to school. We knew that we had to do this correctly, without mishaps because our parents expected it. We understood that the lives of our parents were hard, they came home from work exhausted and that we should not be the cause of any further worry or concern to them.

The winter of 1957 had subdued the land. Everything seemed dull, dismal, dejected. The thermometer reading continued to remain on the freezing point and the people continued to wear grim expressions as they tried to catch buses or trains to get to work in the cold, through the mist and fog. Keeping warm and fending off the flu or the whooping cough were serious preoccupations.

Having recently arrived in England, barely eleven months before, we assumed that the people during winter became glum and unhappy and who could blame them? We were therefore greatly surprised at the beginning of December, when the weather was even harsher, to note a real change in the general mood. The first sign of the coming celebrations was when the local shops were adorned with attractive, multi-coloured, paper decorations. Christmas trees appeared and were being sold outside the shops. These were then put up in living rooms, close to the window so they could be seen from the street. They were covered in attractive paper decorations, tinsel and sometimes tufts of cotton wool to give the effect of snow. Neighbours seemed to be competing on who would have the best Christmas tree in their street. There were other signs of the change of mood. The hitherto glum citizens of London had suddenly and unexpectedly, rediscovered the art of smiling in the midst of winter. The pubs, even more than usual, were doing a brisk trade; people were crowding into the smoke filled public bars, gathering together to drink, to sing and be merry. Light and bitter or a pint of stout was the usual drink for the men, while the ladies often drank gin and tonic. As they imbibed, both men and women usually had cigarettes dangling from the side of their mouths in imitation of their favourite Hollywood stars who had helped to popularise the smoking habit by making it look glamorous in their films. The consumption of beer and spirits gave the merry makers a flushed appearance and added to their sense of goodwill, common brotherhood, friendship and kindness. It was as if people were prepared to forget about the cold weather, the demands of working in factories or offices, paying the never-ending bills for this or that. Christmas was approaching, and they were determined to enjoy themselves in any way that was possible. The change of mood happened so quickly, it was so surprising, and it was so good to notice it.

It wasn't just the effect of drink, there was without a doubt, a change in outlook. People looked happier, they smiled more and greeted you in a friendlier manner. They were brisker, had more purpose and direction. The high roads were full of people looking into shop windows, assessing the goods on sale, pointing and making comments to each other. They shopped more, carrying their goods in boxes and parcels, smiling and looking happy, satisfied and content. They no longer heeded the grim grey weather. Rationing in Britain had come to an end in 1954 and was now only a memory. People had gone from a time of scarcity to a time of plenty. This was boom time Britain, December 1957. The factories and coal mines were in full production. The stocks and shares in the City of London were trading robustly, the export market was thriving and the ports were an immense hive of activity. Only a few months before, the Prime Minister Harold Macmillan had delivered his 'you have never had it so good' speech to the British people in which he proudly declared the economic miracle that the United Kingdom had experienced:

"Go around the country, go to the industrial towns, go to the farms and you will see a state of prosperity such as we have never had in my lifetime – nor indeed in the history of this country."
Harold Macmillan, Prime Minister.
20th July, 1957.

The post war economy had really taken off. There was a huge increase in wages, the standard of living was rising; there was full employment and confidence in the emerging consumer society. But more than anything else, Christmas 1957 was made to feel a little warmer and a little brighter by the velvety voice of Harry Belafonte whose song *Mary's Boy Child*, a harmonisation of traditional carol melody and calypso rhythm, had made it to the top of 'The Official Singles Chart'. During the Christmas period, its sweet melody singing out the Christmas story, could be heard flowing from every juke box in every coffee bar and pub throughout the land. Things were going well, the economy was thriving, rationing was hardly thought about, people had money to spend and Christmas was approaching. It was a time of hope.

Father, who was resilient to both the cold weather and the hostility of the teddy boys, was fast becoming an anglophile and as the great festival of Christmas approached, he felt that he understood the sudden change in the temperament of the people. He said that he had been in England in the Christmas of 1956 and he had seen the same thing.

"The English love Christmas. They love it so much! In Cyprus, the most important thing is to have our Communion at church and listen to the Holy Liturgy but for the English, it is much more. They will eat and drink and buy presents. They will send Christmas cards even to the people that they don't like."

We all laughed at Father's analysis and he felt encouraged to carry on with his amusing presentation of English behaviour at Christmas.

"It is amazing! You will see that the closer you get to Christmas Day, the more they will become excited. They are just like children. They really love Christmas."

He chuckled to himself as he thought about it. Then to our surprise, he made an announcement.

"On Saturday afternoon, we will catch the underground train and go to the West End to see the lights."

"What lights are you talking about, Loizo?"

My mother had not been to the West End and she felt a little confused about the lights that we were going to see.

"The West End is where there are the best shops, the best restaurants, the best of everything in the whole of England. Nicosia, even Athens are nothing in comparison to the West End."

"Let's go now! Let's go now!"

My sister and I became over-excited because it was not often that Father offered to take us out.

"We will go to Trafalgar Square where it is full of pigeons that fly onto your hand to eat food. Now they have put up a giant Christmas tree there and it is full of lights. It is a present from the King and Queen of Norway for the help that the English gave them during the war. But better than this will be the lights and decorations of Regent Street and the shops of Oxford Street. You will like it very much!"

That night, I went to bed thinking of the wonderful day we were going to have in the West End. I was so excited that I could not get to sleep for a long time. My parents in the next room were already fast asleep and I could hear my sister's gentle and regular breathing in the bed opposite mine while I continued to imagine the dazzle of Oxford Street, the shining lights of Regent Street and the giant Christmas tree given by the King and Queen of Norway in a place where pigeons ate out of the palm of your hand.

Father didn't break his promise. One Saturday afternoon, we dressed as smartly as possible, put on our new overcoats, the very first that we had ever possessed and headed for the tube.

Travelling on the underground was another new and extraordinary experience. It was the strangest thing that I had ever seen. The tunnels, so deep under the ground! I felt as if we had entered into some peculiar and unknown place. To me, it was bewildering, confusing and felt like the beginning of an extraordinary adventure.

My excitement grew when as we stood on the platform and as I peered into the darkness of the tunnels at each end, there came a loud screeching, metallic sound, followed by a gush of warm air and then from the darkness of the tunnel, a light hurtling towards us. Within seconds, the train like a dragon with a long tail and with a great roar, entered the station and came to a standstill right on the kerb of the platform. As if by magic, the doors of the carriages opened by themselves for us to enter. When we were safely on, we heard a loud cry from the platform.

"Stand clear of the doors!"

The doors closed and the train, to begin with, moved slowly off, but then, very quickly, gathered speed. It was like a bullet, shooting through the bowels of the earth. It shook! It rattled! It screeched and growled through the darkness far, far, under the ground.

The train was packed with people. Men and women, boys and girls, all dressed in warm clothes, wearing scarves and hats. The seats were all occupied and whenever anybody vacated their place because they had reached their destination, it was immediately occupied by the nearest standing passenger. Most people didn't bother trying to speak over the great noise that the train was making. They sat quietly, usually with blank, impersonal expressions simply because people on the tube don't know each other. Not realising this simple fact, we could not help comparing the pensive attitude of the passengers on the tube with the passengers who travelled on the old rusting bus that went between Stylloi and Varosi, who all knew each other and who saw their journey as an opportunity to laugh and joke, to argue and discuss, to catch up on the latest news and gossip. In comparison, the faces on the tube were quiet, still, thoughtful. Even the children were undemanding and passive as if they knew by instinct that this was a place in which you sat still and quiet. The only sound came from the electric rails and the train moving at great speed through the miles of tunnels that seemed to go on forever.

Every few minutes, the train reached the next station and stopped to allow people to get off and on. Each time I tried to read the names of the stations: Finsbury Park, Arsenal, Hollow Way Road, Caledonian Road, Kings Cross and so on until we at last we arrived at Piccadilly Circus. We alighted from the train and followed Father through the vast caverns crowded with people who moved to and fro in never ending, orderly streams. After climbing some steps and making a turn, we came to a junction that had two electric staircases side by side that moved in opposite directions; one moved upwards and the other moved downwards. This was another unbelievable phenomenon of the world of magic as it seemed to me, known as the London Underground. As we looked up, it appeared that these electric stairways were very long and steep. My father was confident because he had used them before but Mother, Kika and even I, with my love for adventure, felt a little apprehensive at the thought of climbing onto the moving stairs. After some hesitancy, Father led the way again and we nervously followed. Once we had stepped on, we laughed with relief to discover that there was nothing to it. We stood on the escalator, holding firmly on to the moving banister, looking downwards and then upwards, feeling nervous and happy that we had overcome our fear. It carried us up, up, up, all the way to the surface of the earth. How deep we had been! Deep in the deepest cavern imaginable! We were impressed, we were surprised, we were in disbelief at the wonders and mysteries of the London Underground!

We emerged onto the lights of Piccadilly Circus. Immediately, we were struck by the flickering neon lights that covered all the buildings around Piccadilly. The neon signs for 'Coca Cola', 'Bovril', 'Wrigley's' and 'Time for a Guinness' flashed on and off in a variety of luminous bright red, orange, yellow and green colours. In the centre of Piccadilly stood then as now, the famous statue of Eros[1], with wings out spread, balancing lightly on one leg as if in flight and with his arrow aimed towards Shaftsbury Avenue. The red buses of London Transport packed with people, black cabs carrying their passengers and hundreds of cars made their way around the focal point of the statue before taking one of the many exits. The whole area was full of people, young and old, excited, jubilant, out for a good time, to see the lights, to have a drink, to notice and to be noticed; they walked through Piccadilly with loud laughter, eyes that were wide and gay, showing the joy of the young in a place full of the possibility of magic and romance. We were awed by the intensity of the place!

Eventually and with reluctance, we turned our backs onto Piccadilly Circus and walked towards Leicester Square. Here, just a short distance from the illuminations of Piccadilly was another place full of people, lights and activity. In the middle of the square was a small park surrounded by iron railings and at its centre there was a faded statue of William Shakespeare. This statue, unlike the impressive statue of Eros, was hardly noticeable but what really attracted our attention were the many cafés, pubs and cinemas that surrounded the square. Again, we were enthralled by what we saw. The buildings stood high, the huge glass entrances to the cinemas and theatres were full of light and richly carpeted in red or blue. You could see crowds of smartly dressed people patiently waiting to see a show or a film. The cafés and restaurants were also crowded with people out on a Saturday evening, talking and laughing, smoking cigarettes, eating and drinking cups of tea or coffee or even something stronger!

After walking around Leicester Square for a while, we decided it was time to move on. We made our way towards Trafalgar Square, past the National Portrait Gallery on the right and Saint Martin's-in-the-Field opposite on the left. As we entered the square we could not help feeling rather impressed by its grandeur. It was an imposing, imperial representation of the empire, the great power that Britain had once been. There were magnificent buildings with huge Grecian columns around the periphery of the square. Huge statues of generals and kings stood looking seriously into the horizon. With four gigantic sculptures of lions set at its base, a huge column rose in the centre of the brightly lit square and on top of it was mounted the statue of the great Admiral, Lord Nelson who was the victor of the defining Battle of Trafalgar. Alongside the great column were two magnificent fountains, decorated with sculptures of dolphins, mermen and mermaids with water gashing from their mouths. Here was also the great Christmas tree from Norway decorated with hundreds of lights. We gazed and gazed at this oasis, we were impressed, we were awed by what we saw, we felt then that we had indeed come to live in one of the world's greatest cities. Father broke the spell when he tried to give us all a history lesson. He pointed to the column with the great statue on top of it, at the centre of the square.

"That is someone very famous in England. He is a great admiral called Nelson. He fought the French and destroyed their fleet."

Mother looked amused.

"How do you know all this, Loizo," she said jokingly. "Have you been secretly attending school?"

We all laughed at Mother's joke and continued to walk around the square for a little longer.

We carried on walking, winding our way through the maze of London streets, streets brightly lit by thousands of lights from shops and buildings. It seemed like a flood of light that turned night into day, illuminating our way, enabling us to explore and discover the wonders of the metropolis.

We eventually made our way to Regent Street where there was a splendid and illuminated display of Christmas decorations. When we first came upon it, we were overwhelmed. It was beyond comparison, we had never seen anything like it ever before. It was as if we had entered a magical land that was full of a beautiful glow that came from all directions. It was like El Dorado, it was like the Land of Oz, it was Aladdin's cave; it was a place that was full of promise and possibilities. We looked on in disbelief at the wonderful sight. The whole street glittered with brightly lit up shop windows full of stylish goods presented in an artistic and creative manner with life-like mannequins dressed in the most glamorous and stylish clothes that you could imagine and whose eyes seemed to follow you around everywhere you went. There were all kinds of shops selling everything that you could dream of. The best clothes of the latest trend, the shoes of the finest leather, sparkling jewellery, heavy and comfortable furniture crafted for the rich and the famous or just for the admiration of those who could not afford them who were merely passing by.

The street was full of people, people were everywhere, walking along the pavements, crossing the roads in between the moving cars; they were entering and exiting from shops and cafés; ladies in fur coats who looked like film stars and gentlemen in smart suits and trilby hats walked around carrying parcels of Christmas shopping. Children glowed with excitement as they gathered to look into the brightly lit up shops crammed full of dolls, teddy bears and miniature prams for the girls and Hornby train sets with engine models of the Flying Scotsman for the boys. I looked at these wonderful toys, feeding my eyes with their enticing allure and in particular, I looked at the model of the Flying Scotsman and I felt a great and powerful desire to have it. My father looked at me and probably guessed what I was thinking. He smiled warmly at me without saying anything. We then continued our walk, joining the endless stream of people traversing along the pavement at a slow pace while cars and buses, packed with people and shiny black cabs with passengers sitting comfortably in the rear headed for their destinations along the wide curving road.

Above all the commotion and traffic, fixed in mid-air, were models of air balloons in bright, vibrant colours. We were so captivated; we felt that we were experiencing something extraordinary, extraordinary because nowhere in the world could there have been such a wonderful display. The decorations extended along the whole length of Regent Street; from Piccadilly Circus at one end, all the way to Oxford Circus at the other. Of all the pleasing, jovial and artistic Christmas displays, the air balloons that decorated Regent Street during the Christmas period of 1957 were for me at that time, the most intensely eye-catching, exciting and pleasing. No other display had ever evoked in me such awe, amazement or amusement!

Long after the event, we continued to talk about our day out to the West End; Trafalgar Square with its great columns and fountains gushing with water, Piccadilly Circus full of multi-coloured dazzling lights and at its centre, Eros, in flight and with his bow drawn ready to shoot his arrow. Most of all, we talked about Regent Street with its unforgettable, multi-coloured air balloons, decorating the length and breadth of its skyline. Our day out had been wonderful, truly entertaining and memorable. It certainly gave us an inkling of how grand and magnificent the metropolis of London really is, like a huge organism with its millions of people busily working and living their own individual lives, each one unique and different, under its broad and often times, blustery skies.

1. Statue of Eros – this is the work of Alfred Gilbert. It was made between 1885—1893 and it was cast in aluminium and bronze. Its official title is 'The Shaftesbury Memorial Fountain' and it was erected to honour and commemorate the philanthropic works of Lord Shaftesbury, the famous Victorian politician and philanthropist. Originally, the statue was meant to represent Anteros, the god of selfless love in the classical pantheon which can be equated with the concept of Christian Charity and appropriate for the purpose of the statue to honour Lord Shaftesbury. The statue, however, has come to be commonly referred to almost from the beginning, as Eros, the god of sensual love and inappropriate for the purpose of commemorating philanthropic works. Ironically, Eros, the popular name for the statue proved to be more in keeping with the sex trade that nearby Soho was associated with for many years in the 20th century. Shaftesbury Memorial Fountain. Wikipedia.

The Crises

It wasn't long after our arrival in England that we began to feel more settled and even satisfied that we had come to live in London. It's true, the sun didn't shine very much, it was cold and it often rained but there were regular busses that took you to work; there were doctors and hospitals if you didn't feel well; the children went to school; there was the Labour Exchange to find you work if you were unemployed and provided financial help to tide you over until you had employment. We liked England with its order and stability, its certainty and assuredness. We liked living amongst the English people, who on the whole, had welcomed us or, at least, they allowed us to get on with our lives unhindered, despite the fact that in Cyprus, EOKA was conducting a bloody campaign against the British Army in the name of Enosis.

We feared that when English people read newspapers and listened to the radio about the attacks on British soldiers and how the Greek Cypriots wanted an end to British rule, they would link us, the Cypriots living with them in London, with the awful events that were occurring in Cyprus. This was a difficult, anxious and nervous time. We suffered some very disturbing experiences, experiences that were deeply demoralising: I had been made a scapegoat in class because my picture of Guy De Fawkes resembled Archbishop Makarios, I had been verbally abused and physically threatened by a man on the street who had called me a Greek bastard, my father had been attacked at a bus stop by racist thugs, we had been verbally abused while doing our weekly shopping at the market by persons who were complete strangers to us. It was humiliating; it was a blow to our pride as worthwhile people; it was a blow to our self-esteem.

However, as unsavoury as all this may seem, the episodes of abuse were in fact, thankfully few and isolated. There was no pogrom, no wide spread attacks on our community. There wasn't anything like the dreadful events of the Septemvriana[1] that befell the Rum of Istanbul in September 1955. Thank Heaven the British do not have this trait in their character. They regard the use of pogrom – the attack of the majority against a defenceless minority – as an unmanly, cowardly and extreme act. The British sense of fair play has never allowed the thugs and extremists to dictate policy in relation to the ethnic minorities who have been constantly protected by not only the law but also by the goodwill of the people.

Therefore, as a little boy during the late fifties, I walked to school in safety and I had English friends who played with me and included me in their company. The attitude of the English people with whom we lived and worked was generally friendly and kind, kind enough to help us to forget the few unpleasant experiences we had had with racists and for our wounded pride to heal quickly and for our confidence to return.

We were managing to overcome many of our problems of settling into our new homeland. Unfortunately, the crises in Cyprus wouldn't go away. Greek Cypriot newspapers were being posted to London, full of the news about what was going on in Cyprus. The exchange of letters with family was also another source of information for London Cypriots about the crises. When people met, whatever the venue, whether it was church, café or in each other's houses, the subject of the conversation was always the crises:

What will happen with the EOKA struggle?
The people demanded Enosis. Would they be successful?
What about the Turkish Cypriots?
Could they be forced to live under the conditions Enosis?
Would they ever accept such a fate?
Independence. Wouldn't that be better?
The Greek and Turkish Cypriots, could they ever make peace
and work together again?

There were many questions that were being asked. At the time there was no alternative vision of what Cyprus could become. The blinkers of nationalism were worn by each community in Cyprus and not understanding the consequences, made no attempt to remove them. The furnace of nationalism had been lit and the fires of hatred had been stoked until carnage, chaos and confusion were unleashed upon the people of Cyprus. Any voice of reason had been hardly audible, any peaceful alternative had been ridiculed and any talk of compromise was smothered at birth. Yet, the signs of the impending disaster were there to be clearly seen. I am thinking, in particular, about the events in Tilliryia in the north west of Cyprus in August 1964, when the Greek Cypriot National Guard laid siege to the Turkish Cypriot enclave of Kokkina from where they had been smuggling arms from Turkey. Turkey intervened with its powerful air force. It used napalm bombs in its attacks against Greek Cypriot targets and there were both civilian and military casualties. This event, sadly, did not teach any useful lessons to the Cypriots. At this point, there was no political person on either side who was courageous or wise enough to come forward with a new peaceful vision which the two opposing communities could begin to think about.

The 1964 bombardment was the clearest sign; it was the writing on the wall, it was a bloody foretaste of the disaster that was to follow. This event, which should have encouraged a different way of trying to solve the Cyprus problem, was instead used by fanatical nationalists to sow the seeds of further hate and distrust. This was like the first act of a tragedy and the gullible Cypriots were the tragic heroes who through their hubris would continue to suffer an unhappy fate.

At the time, I was a pupil in secondary school in London. There was a fair number of both Greek Cypriot and Turkish Cypriot children who attended the school. We were friends in every way. We supported the same football clubs of the English League; we spoke about our school subjects; we looked out for each other in the playground when facing bullies; we ate together at lunch time, many of the Turkish Cypriot children could speak Cypriot Greek and we all attended a special class to learn English in which the teacher had thought that when we communicated with each other, we were speaking in 'Cypriotish'. In fact, if you think about it, you could say this with some degree of truth because the Greek and Turkish dialects of Cyprus, which share many features, are quite different to the standard Greek and Turkish Languages. So, to those who didn't know Cyprus, we were the same and we were speaking 'Cypriotish'. This amused us and made us feel closer together.

But on the subject of Cyprus and what was happening there, we were at a loss on how to tackle this issue simply because we had all been fed the nationalist hatred by our elders who were bankrupt of the alternatives to nationalism. We had never heard of anyone expounding ideas about sharing, working together, celebrating our common culture, building a new common motherland called Cyprus. So, we argued, argued about which side was stronger, who was going to win the war, who was going to rule Cyprus. The Greek Cypriot students and the Turkish Cypriot students, who had so much in common with each other, far from their homes in Cyprus, in their new land, bickered, threatened and expostulated while their English friends looked on bewildered and amused at how such good friends from the same place could laugh and joke with each other one minute and then the next minute, argue heatedly, vigorously and passionately with each other.

Ignorance and innocence had the better of us; we didn't understand why the people in Cyprus were divided; we didn't understand what the consequences of division would be; we didn't understand that there was a better way forward; as children, nobody explained to us that there are more things in common between the Greek Cypriots and Turkish Cypriots than with any other people or country including Greece and Turkey; so we argued with each other, just like our people in Cyprus:

"Cyprus belongs to the Greeks because we were there first!"

"Who says you were there first! The Turks ruled Cyprus for four hundred years!"

"The Greeks are the majority. We are 80% of the population."

"It doesn't matter, Cyprus is closer to Turkey than it is to Greece and a long time ago, it was even joined to Turkey."

We knew a lot of facts, or, what we thought were facts and the silly arguments went on. In the playground, my friend Shakir Hussain, a fellow Cypriot and a brilliant football player, told me that the Turkish Air Force was going to bomb the hell out of the Greek Cypriots.

"They're going to fly over Cyprus. They've got hundreds of jets. They're going to bomb the hell out of you."

"Let them try if they can," I shouted back, "the Greek Army will be in Constantinople in twenty-four hours!"

We believed this. Each of us thought that this was the best solution. We had heard this from our parents; we had heard this from our teachers in Cyprus; we had heard this from our wise politicians. Even in England, the cycle of mistrust and hatred was being perpetuated, but at least in England, it could never be more than an argument; in Cyprus, the alienation between the two communities would become much more intense. Cyprus became a house divided against its self.

A tribal war ensued; rape, murder, massacre and destruction were inflicted against each other. This was the work of our own hands. How strange, how inconceivable, how foolish that the people of Cyprus, who had gained their independence in 1960, pledged their loyalty not to the land of their birth but to the two so-called motherlands, Greece or Turkey, places where most Cypriots had never visited at that time and knew very little about. How absurd was the desire and political ambition to have your state but to wish it to be abolished and for your country to be under the rule of another power. I cannot think of any other country in the world that has made such a choice. History is full of examples about how nations and people often fight gallantly, bravely, with courage and conviction to gain their liberty and, once achieved, to guard that liberty as if it was the most precious thing in the world. But the Cypriots, having achieved independence for the first time in their history, wanted to give it away, as if it was a thing of no value, of no consequence, an undesirable, unimportant and unwanted privilege. Of all the absurd, political decisions that have sometimes been mistakenly made by people in history, the decision to willingly give up your country to another must be the most absurd of all! It is absurd! Absurd in the extreme! It is the absurdity of all absurdities!

1- The Istanbul Pogrom, 6-7 September, 1955. Greeks call this dreadful episode 'The Septemvriana'. It refers to the events that were organised by the Turkish Army's Tactical Mobilisation Force. The events were set in motion by the news that the Turkish Consulate in Thesaloniki that was also the house in which Kemal Attaturk, the founder of modern Turkey had been born in, had suffered damage in a bomb attack. The person responsible was a Turkish security guard who had been arrested and had confessed his crime. The Turkish media, however, reported the bombing of the consulate but had deliberately omitted the part played by the Turkish security guard and entirely blamed the event on the Greeks. This deliberate disinformation led to the well-planned and orchestrated riots in which the Greek community of Istanbul was savagely attacked by a frenzied Turkish mob resulting in death and destruction. After this event, in fear of further attacks and persecution, the Greek community of Istanbul, who were the descendants of the founders of the city, fled to Greece and other countries, bringing to an end the thousands of years of Greek civilisation in what is now modern Turkey. Septemvriana. Alfred de Zayas, Geneva School of Diplomacy. Futurista, 2014.

Speaking and Listening

Even as a young man, I had realised that living in London was an enriching, worthwhile and positive experience. Though as a child, I had stood feeling alone and isolated in that classroom where I had been hit by my teacher or was taunted by a passer-by in a busy street in North London, these experiences did not embitter me. To counteract these isolated events, I had innumerable constructive and sometimes brilliant experiences in school. My teachers were mostly very kind, helpful and caring and it is these people that I thank for not allowing the seeds of disillusion to grow or to flourish in my mind. The one rotten apple at the bottom of the barrel could not change my feelings about how truly wonderful my teachers had been.

School for me had been a place of interest, creativity, development and where I was able to achieve my potential. I certainly, very quickly, picked up the ability to communicate in English. In my first year of school in Cyprus, I was taught to read phonically and soon after when we had arrived in England, I used those skills to decipher the English alphabet and to embark on my interest in reading that has delighted me throughout my life. My love of reading stories I know, harked back to the folk tales my grandmother narrated to my sister and me some years before, in our village in Cyprus. Folk tales are the same the world over and this was a strong link between my past in Cyprus and my boyhood experiences in England. The more English I learnt, the more I grew in confidence.

My sister had learnt English fairly quickly, but she was not as fluent as me. At fifteen, she left school and started working in the same factory as my mother. In fact, she often complained that it was unfair that she was not given the opportunity to study and to reach her potential. What happened to her also happened to thousands of other Cypriot young women. The Cypriots who came to England in the 1950s and early 1960s, came with the attitude that the role of a young woman is to marry, bear children, to be of help to her husband and at the same time, have a full-time job. Many felt that there wasn't any need to educate a girl, for there would not be any use for this education. This was a crude, naive and very narrow-minded attitude. In time, for the Cypriot community, this attitude

146

changed but it did not change soon enough to benefit my sister Kika. She worked with mother; she was a teenage bride, bore children before she was even twenty years of age and then worked very hard to raise them. She was trapped by a blind tradition.

Our parents, who were loving and kind, were also trapped in their perception of what was right for their daughter and even now, in England, there are other ethnic communities who continue to perceive their young women as objects that are owned and who must obey customs and traditions from far way. When these young women sometimes dare to refute the unwritten laws of their communities, they become outcasts and sometimes even worse. My experience was in sharp contrast to that of my sister. Sadly, we were not treated as being of equal importance. Boys were elevated and encouraged while girls were subjugated and limited in their aspirations.

Having learnt to speak English quite fluently and in addition having acquired the ability to read and write with some accuracy, my importance in the family grew, grew substantially for an eleven-year-old boy and even though my sister had also made progress with her reading and writing in English, her abilities and skills were unfairly dismissed by our parents. It was to me that my father looked to for help when dealing with the English officialdom. He hadn't learnt English beyond a few spoken phrases and it seemed inevitable that I was soon to become his interpreter and translator. This included the reading and response to letters relating to tax, social benefits, housing and other such issues. I was given the responsibility for writing letters or completing important forms. I always accompanied my father to the Labour Exchange on occasions when he was seeking employment or sorting out issues of tax or benefits. Mother also used me as an interpreter usually at the doctors or for her hospital appointments. I remember how after mother's examination, the friendly GP looked at me with an admiring smile, offered me a sweet and said,

"You're doing a fine job, Master Loizou, a really fine job. Well done!"

Of no less importance to my language development was when Father, on a regular basis, asked me to interpret the BBC news as it was being presented on the television. I do not know whether Father had an interest in the news or whether it was because he felt that this exercise was helping me acquire important language skills, but it became our habit that whenever possible, we would settle down together in front of the television and I then attempted to perform an instant translation of the news. This was one of the few enjoyable father and son activities that he and I engaged in. I am quite certain that having only recently acquired a fairly fluent ability in spoken English, the accuracy of my translations might have been found wanting. My father would sit comfortably on his armchair and sometimes smiled in a knowing amused manner. It was probably at the wild inaccuracies and exaggerations of my translations. There was never any criticism of my abilities and I am certain that indeed, this exercise was intended by my father to help me with both my Greek and English.

My fluency in both these languages gave me a respect in the family that had come to rely on my language skills to make sense of British Society. Not only did they call upon me to interpret the language but also to explain what politicians were saying on television or the action and dialogue of films and even the jokes in comedy shows on television. Our favourite comedians were Charlie Drake and Norman Wisdom whose humour was easy to follow for my parents because much of it was based on farce. We laughed heartily at Charlie Drake stumbling off ladders into pots or buckets full of water or paint; we laughed at Norman Wisdom in his cloth cap, creating a crisis for Mr Grimsdale at every turn. We sat around the television on Saturday nights enjoying films and shows like many other ordinary families. This was in a sense an initiation into British culture and we were unknowingly very keen receptors. My parents were forever trying to work out what was going on, what was being said.

"Tell me what he is saying, Fotaki. What are they going to do? What is going to happen?" they asked me every five minutes.

Sometimes, my sister and I really protested because we found the constant interruptions from our parents prevented us from enjoying the programmes. This didn't stop them from persisting!

I had a sense even then that my parents were deeply interested in this new place that they had come to, that they were curious and inquisitive to know about its nature and spirit but recognised that language was a difficult obstacle, a barrier which prevented most people like them, who had had very little formal education, from finding a true understanding of British society. So, I became their ears and their tongue, helping them in their challenging new life, in the great metropolis of London.

In addition to this, my visits to the Labour Exchange with my father where I interpreted questions about work skills or previous employments, gave me a sense of adult concerns about work and the importance of earnings.

One day when we were sitting quietly at home, in response to my questions about why we were yet again going to the Labour Exchange, my father tried to explain the importance of this organisation for working people. He settled back into his chair as if he had a lot to speak about and that it would take some time to do so. He spoke in a simple and direct manner as if he was speaking with an adult:

"Fotaki," he spoke with warmth and affection, "we have come from a beautiful homeland. Cyprus is a place that has been blessed by God with many gifts. It has mountains covered with forests, it has a rich soil so that crops grow in abundance…"

"So why did we leave Cyprus and come to England, Father?"

"I was about to explain. You see, the land and the wealth always seemed to belong to the very rich people who were never happy to share and who always wanted more and more wealth. People like us had next to nothing. We could only sell our labour. We had to work incredibly hard and receive very little in return. Sometimes, I worked as a labourer, a *hamali*[1], loading and unloading cargo ships in Famagusta Port or I mixed cement and carried bricks on a building site, burning in the heat of the summer sun and not having enough money at the end of the week for our basic needs. Sometimes, there was not enough food in the house and your mother and I went without food so you and your sister could have something and not go to bed feeling hungry."

I looked at him and wondered whether Grandmother had judged him harshly when she often called him a 'waster' and that Mother would always be unhappy with such a husband. However, I still remained uncertain about what all this had to do with the Labour Exchange. I remained silent and attentive. He continued:

"The problem was that working people in Cyprus had almost no rights. If you were unskilled you could be laid off a job and then there would be no money for the family. This happened to me many times. Perhaps for a while, I managed to find work building a villa for some rich man. After a few months, when the job was completed, the contractor dismissed us until he had another project but this might take months."

He sometimes paused as if to reflect on the details of what he was saying and then, when he was satisfied, he resumed his explanation.

"In England, the working people are better organised. If you don't have a job, the Labour Exchange will help you to find one and if you have no money, they will help you until you can earn some for yourself. That is why we go to the Labour Exchange. It is to find work so that we can live. One day, Fotaki, when you are an adult and have a family, you will realise that to have a job is the most important thing in your life. A man without employment is not a man. How can you live not knowing whether you can feed your children? How many times can you go to your relatives who might not have very much themselves and ask them for help? How many times can you ask the grocer for credit? You begin to feel ashamed and useless. You begin to feel like a person without dignity. The Labour Exchange helps me find work and that is why I came to England. I am here to work."

He looked at me expecting me to understand the plight of the working man in Cyprus and in comparison, the practical advantages that working people had in England.

Translating the television news for my father had a long-term impact upon me. Through this process, I became intensely interested in current affairs. I wanted to know what was going on in England and in the world. I followed news stories from the Parliament and began to understand that there were two main political parties, the Labour Party and the Conservative Party, and they were always at loggerheads with each other. In the conversations that I had with my father and which usually occurred after the early evening news, he explained their difference in a simple and lucid manner:

"Fotaki," he addressed me affectionately, "the Labour Party is for the ordinary working people like us. They want to give us better conditions at work. They want to have a better health service and build new schools for the children. The Conservatives are for the rich people who want even more than what they have already, just like the rich people in Cyprus, who build fine villas and drive expensive cars manufactured in England and who don't give a damn if the ordinary people around them are going hungry. They think that they are the masters and the purpose for the poor in society is to serve them."

There was some anger in his voice when he had said this. I looked on, waiting for him to continue.

"It is unfair that some people have so much while others, even if they work day and night, have very little. Everybody needs a chance to have a better life, but in Cyprus, the poor get poorer while the rich have everything that they like. It is very wrong!"

He felt that Harold Wilson was a politician[2] who could be relied upon to help ordinary working people. Father always voted for Labour and he was overjoyed when in 1967, Harold Wilson made his famous visit to Moscow.

"He is not like the Conservative politicians. The people can trust Wilson because he is always trying to help the workers. He is friends with Russia because he is also socialist. He is the leader of the Labour Party who will always try to help working people and they don't care if you are black, white or Cypriot."

Thus, I began to think about party politics from quite an early age. Another great influence was *The Times* newspaper with its division of the news into *Home News*, *European News* and *World News* categories. I began to follow with increasing clarity and understanding the threads in stories that held together the changing circumstances and changing fortunes of countries and political personalities – The Kennedys, Fidel

Castro, The Bay of Pigs, The Cuba Missile Crises, The Six Day War, Vietnam, Cyprus – an endless list of events and stories presented in the newspapers like the never ending stories of Shaharazade or the soap operas that fascinate modern television audiences. This interest in current affairs that grabbed my attention at such a young age became a compulsion that I still experience. A daily read of at least one serious newspaper is a must for me and if time allows, a further reading of international news from the internet. Little did my father realise that when he requested me to translate the BBC evening news on television, that one day this habit would turn me into an insatiable consumer of the news.

1. *Hamali*: this word is used throughout the Middle East. It is probably of Arabic origin. It is the name given to porters, or labourers who carry loads from one place to another. The word also describes someone without education or trade.
2. Harold Wilson was British Prime Minister between 1964–1970 and 1974–1976.

The Duveen Gallery

As a sixteen-year-old boy, I began to show awareness and some appreciation of the English teenage culture around me and in particular, the unique cultural advantages of living in the capital city of the United Kingdom. The British Museum must count as one of those huge cultural advantages. How could anyone with an interest in history and culture not be impressed with the epic treasures contained within its wide halls?

On my first visit, I stood by the tall iron gates of the museum and looked upon the imposing facade of Ionic columns. This was a Greek temple built in the classical style. It seemed as if some holy shrine dedicated to Zeus had been magically transplanted from the vale of Arcadia and brought to these northern shores to house treasures from the four corners of the earth. From every point of view, I felt that this was a very special place, even though I did not exactly know what I expected to find inside this museum. As it turned out, I was not going to be disappointed.

With dozens of other visitors, I walked along the broad paved pathway leading to the stone steps. As I approached the portico, I gazed up in wonder at the massive fluted columns that supported the pediment and the frieze with its fine sculptures depicting the ancient gods of Olympus. For the first time but not the last, I entered through the massive doors of this incredible temple dedicated to the history and achievements of mankind, not realising that this would be the beginning of a long and loving relationship that I would have with this very special institution.

The first area of interest that I wondered into was the hall containing the Egyptian collection. There were mummies of men and women, of boys and girls, there were even mummies of cats and dogs. The gallery displayed a huge number of statues in stiff postures, gazing blankly into space. Then there was the Rosetta Stone, a slab of black granite with Egyptian hieroglyphics, Assyrian cuneiform and Greek letters neatly carved upon it. The three texts carved on the stone corresponded in meaning with each other. This was of great interest to me because we had studied at school about the importance of the Rosetta Stone and how it had enabled Jean-Francois Champillion and Thomas Young, two brilliant

19th century scholars, to decipher the as yet unknown ancient languages of Egypt and Assyria by comparing them with the familiar ancient Greek. As I stood there, I tried to use my knowledge of Greek to read something from the stone but to no avail, for it all seemed strange and unreadable. I could not make any sense of it and so, I moved on, strolling through the wide halls crammed to the brim with treasures from other lands.

How could it be, I asked myself, that so many artefacts could have been brought from the four corners of the earth to reside in the heart of London? The answer to this question was at that particular moment in time, uncertain and unclear to me. I also experienced, even from my earliest visits, that despite the magnificence of the British Museum, Egyptian mummies, statues and indeed the other display pieces were somehow in an alien environment, far from home, out of context.

I continued to stroll through the halls of the museum and went from the Egyptian gallery to the halls that contained the collection from Greece. The stiff and lifeless style of Egyptian sculpture gave way to life-like and idealised human forms of classical or Hellenistic art.

At the entrance of a great hall, I noticed the bust of Perikles the Athenian. The bust was familiar to me from pictures in history books. This famous sculpted portrait of white marble with the name of Perikles Xanthippou boldly carved at the base, depicted the famous statesman as having fine, noble features, with a full curly beard and wearing the helmet of an Athenian hoplite. I could not fail to notice that most visitors barely glanced at it as they entered the main hall of Greek exhibits, but I was drawn to it because I recognised this sculpture from pictures in history books and I knew the name of the man it represented. I was familiar with the knowledge that this man was one of the great personalities of ancient Greece.

I stood before the bust of Perikles and gazed upon his countenance with the feeling that this was the image of a very special man. The large eyes that seemed to gaze into the distance, the hair curling out of the rim of the hoplite helmet, the curled, full beard of a philosopher gave him the look of an ideal and charismatic leader. He was imposing, handsome and wise. It was indeed strange that I should have had such an emotional response to the image of Periklis because at the time, I had only an inkling of his achievements. I knew that it was he who commissioned the building of the Parthenon and the unique sculptures that were going to adorn it. Later, I discovered that Periklis worked very hard to make Athens the most important city state in Greece and he would have achieved much more had he not suffered an untimely death during the fateful plague that had struck the city during the early stages of the Peloponnisian War. The plague eventually proved to be disastrous for Athens. At the centre of his political thinking was that the ordinary citizen of Athens was able to take on civic responsibility, debate the policies of the state and in time of war, take up arms to defend the city.

If the noble Periklis, who had achieved so much for his city, could speak to the Greeks of today, what would he say? I am certain that he would admonish the Greeks over many issues and perhaps like a school master complain that we have not achieved the great potential that was expected of us but most of all, he would have been truly horrified that so many art treasures from Greece had been looted and stolen, including so many of the sculptures that he himself, as the leading statesman of Athens, had commissioned and that these were now in the possession of other people. He most certainly would have wondered how it was possible for a race of people like the Greeks who had proved themselves intelligent, wise and brave and who had achieved great heights in their civilisation, to now find themselves in the dismal circumstances of today. He would have thought about the glory that was Greece and would have wept at the great failure that Greece has become! How could the Greeks of today explain to the great statesman, the confusion and failings of the modern Greek state. Imagine the disappointment that he would feel.

I gradually moved on from the marble image of Periklis into what I discovered to be the Duveen Gallery that had been purpose built to house the marbles of the Parthenon.

As a sixteen-year-old boy, I understood very little about the great achievement that these works of art represented but even so, when I looked at the statue of the reclining god, or at the figures of the Lapiths and Centaurs or the formation of cavalry riding on to the Pan Athenian Festival, I was awestruck by the beauty, the natural appearance and the feeling of movement forever captured in those stones. The sculptured riders of the frieze, forever young, forever confident, forever strong, riding on in their cavalry formation; the Lapiths and Centaurs forever locked in a never-ending battle, all of them, oblivious to the passing of time, while from one generation to the next, people looked on in wonder and admiration.

I left the museum on that day feeling that I had made a great discovery. Here was the primary evidence that would feed my passion for ancient history. The marbles were inspiring and wonderful to behold. They had stimulated my love for classical history and that has remained with me. These sculptures gave me pride in my Greek heritage and I can say without hesitation that the first time I saw the Parthenon marbles has remained an unforgettable experience.

Many years later, when I had the opportunity to visit the Acropolis of Athens, I found myself standing with a group of tourists from England, listening to the tourist guide who was describing to us the architectural and artistic merits of the Parthenon. Perhaps, I was the only person amongst the group who noticed the change in her voice; perhaps I might have even imagined it but I felt as I continued to listen to her description of the ancient temple, her voice had taken on a poetic quality proclaiming to us, her listeners and to the world beyond, that here on the Acropolis, in the shadow of Athena's temple was and continues to be the beating heart of Greece. Her final words referred to the Parthenon marbles and what she said epitomised what every Greek person feels. I clearly remember her words that were full of emotion as she spoke:

"The Parthenon marbles," she said, "are unlike any other treasure produced by our ancient forefathers. The very soul of what is best about Greek civilisation is in the fibre of the marbles. While these holy stones are held captive in a far-off land, Greece itself remains a captive…"

Her words had touched my heart and I could not but shed some tears there on the Acropolis, the holy hill of Athens and to feel more strongly than ever that the Parthenon marbles should be immediately returned to their rightful owners, the people of Greece.

It is worth to briefly note how the Parthenon marbles came to be in England rather than in their country of origin.

The marbles in the Duveen Gallery of the British Museum were an integral part of the Parthenon and the Acropolis of Athens until Thomas Elgin, otherwise known by his title Lord Elgin, removed numerous pieces of sculpture from the temple. Some of the pieces were crudely cut away from the building without consideration for the damage that this action caused. This was undoubtedly an act of vandalism that cannot be defended.

Greece at the time was in the last few years of Ottoman occupation and Elgin, who was British Ambassador at Constantinople, had obtained a 'firman' or 'permit' from the Sultan. This document has been used as an argument for the legality of Elgin's act of vandalism. The Greeks, however, have argued that the legality of the 'firman' is in question and that Elgin had committed an act of theft but that at the time, they were powerless to prevent it.

Since that time, Greek governments have frequently requested that the Parthenon marbles should be returned but the British Government, which had purchased the marbles from Lord Elgin in 1816, refused to return these statues to their place of origin.[1] It does not surprise me that there has been a very strong support amongst intellectuals in United Kingdom for the return of the marbles. Intelligent people always have a sensitive understanding of what is right and what is just. This was very early on given a voice by the poet and Philhellene Lord Byron who in his verses from *Child Harold* comments on this subject:

> Dull is the eye that weeps not to see,
> Thy walls defaced, thy mouldering shrines removed,
> By British hands, which it had best behoved,
> To guard those relics ne'er to be restored.
> Cursed be the hour when from their isle they roved,
> And once again thy hapless bosom gored,
> And snatche'd thy shrinking gods to northern climes abhored![2]

~

As a school boy and even later as a student teacher, I regularly visited the British Museum, enjoying its unique treasures. Ignorantly, I had not really thought much about the debate concerning the return of the marbles. How I became more interested and then supported the idea of the return happened inadvertently: It was when I visited the church of the Apostle Andreas in Kentish Town. I had gone there to arrange for the Baptism of my little daughter Louisa. The Bishop, who seemed an enigmatic personality, had a copy of *The Times* and following his discovery that I was a teacher, he seemed eager to engage in conversation regarding a particular article that referred to the return of the marbles to Greece.

"What do you think about this issue? Should not the British return the marbles?"

It was the first time I was presented with this question. Of course, I had respect for the Bishop and I did not want to appear ignorant about such a subject. I managed, on the spur of the moment, to stammer an answer.

"I think they are unique sculptures… I have seen them several times in the British Museum…and the British really do look after them and value them from a scholarly point of view… But they do belong to Greece, they are a part of Greek Heritage… They should be returned."

I felt fairly satisfied with the answer that I gave to his unexpected question. He seemed pleased with my response and from that moment, I began to take an almost compulsive interest in the debate. I read every article in the newspapers related to this subject and more recently, I have been looking at documents on the internet. Now more than any other time, I really do feel, that with the inauguration of a world class museum in Athens, which has been acclaimed as an architectural master piece, the marbles must be returned to their place of origin.

However, the debate goes on without much hope that the Greek people will successfully retrieve their stolen national treasures at any point in the near future. For the Greeks, the return of the marbles is a national cause, an emotional need, a fulfilment of justice. For successive British Governments, it has been something to joke about. On the 22nd June 2011, Andrew George, the Liberal Democrat M.P. for St Ives, asked David Cameron, the British Prime Minister a question about the Parthenon marbles:

"…does the Prime Minister not agree that we have something which would help regenerate the Greek economy and put to right a 200-year wrong – and that is to give the marbles back."

Cameron ridiculed the idea, saying that Britain was not going to 'lose its marbles'[3].

The valuable and brave ally that had stood by Britain in its hour of need during the darkest period of the Second World War was mocked, dismissed and laughed at in its endeavours to reclaim its stolen art treasures that are an important part of its national heritage. Stolen art treasures not only from Greece but also from other places that had been looted during the years of imperialism, when some countries felt that they had the right to take whatever they wanted from the subjected peoples of the world.

1. The Parthenon Sculptures. Facts and Figures. The British Museum.
2. Lord Byron. *Selected Poems.* Penguin Classics.2006.
3. David Cameron rejects call to return Parthenon marbles to Greece. *The Guardian.* Helene Molholland. 22nd June, 2011.

Mrs Evens and Mr Ward

By the time I had reached secondary school, I was very fluent and articulate in English. I could speak, read and write English as well as any English boy of my age. This enabled me to compete successfully in every aspect of school life. School, despite the racist attitude of one or two teachers that I had encountered along the way, had always remained an exciting place for me. I was encouraged by my mother, who, despite the fact that she could hardly speak English and had a full-time job to contend with, turned up at parents' evenings to find out about my progress. My mother was fascinated by the thought that I was attending an English school in the capital of England. She had hardly attended school and she quite naturally wanted it for my sister and me. On her visits to my school, she was always greatly impressed by the large Victorian building with its large wooden doors and high windows. She called it a palace of education. The wide corridors lined with shining ceramic tiles; the halls with waxed parquet floors; the electric lighting hung from high ceilings and the radiators on every wall that heated the whole school were for her, a source of great satisfaction.

"The children matter in this country! This is a good place where the people care about what happens to their children."

Mother was full of praise for the wonderful country we had come to, having temporarily forgotten about how Father had been attacked by thugs on his way home from work and how in the streets, some people uttered rude, hostile, xenophobic comments directed at us.

As Mother looked at the shelves of books in the classrooms and the display work of the children on the walls, I am certain that she felt that the good in the place that we had made our home far exceeded the bad.

I sat at her side, interpreting her questions into English and my teachers' comments into Greek. Sometimes my teachers joked with me.

"Are you sure, you are telling your mum what I am saying?"

I looked at them and smiled, knowing that I was only being teased.

I had a great love for school and I was a very hard-working student. The old habit of listening to stories first from my grandmother in Cyprus and later, when I'd learnt to read stories from books widely available to me from the school library, sharpened my appetite for English. My reading at school had already evolved and developed into a serious passion. I sensed my love for novels and poems even as a thirteen or fourteen-year-old.

I was very fortunate that I had teachers who inspired me. One such teacher was Mrs Evens. She was a Welsh lady who seemed very old, grand and even aristocratic. She dressed in the finery of the Edwardian era and appeared in every sense impressive to those around her. Her warmth was like a powerful magnet drawing us to her, enabling her to guide us through the reading of *Pygmalion* by George Bernard Shaw or *Macbeth* by William Shakespeare. Her sensitive interpretations, her ability to make us understand the stories, the themes and the language of literature were important moments in my growing love for books. How amusing I had found her reading of Eliza Doolittle and how thought inspiring were her lessons on accent and class! Mrs Evens was always full of praise for my reading and writing. She often displayed my work on the classroom display board. For both my first and second year at secondary school, she awarded me the prize for the most progress in English. For both the fourth and fifth years, I was awarded the English prize for being top of the class in that subject. Most of all, Mrs Evens tried to teach us important values in life.

"Being polite, well mannered, honest, hardworking and possessing a good education will greatly help your advancement in society!"

I can hear her words as if she had just uttered them. She often said this to us, particularly if we were not getting on with our work. It was a gentle reprimand, reminding us of what we had to lose if we did not listen to her instructions. She really cared for her students and wanted to give her guidance for their benefit, well-being and progress.

Mr Ward was the Head of English at Highbury Grove School at the time when I was studying there for my 'A' level GCEs. He was admired by his students. He had an imposing Hollywood appearance, something like Charlton Heston in his role as Moses in *The Ten Commandments* with a tanned complexion, steel grey, curly hair and a voice that became melodious when he spoke about a favourite poem or a play. He was a Cambridge graduate, a master of his subject. We, his students, knew that he could recite from texts and the beauty of his recital from the opening lines of *Paradise Lost* or from *The Canterbury Tales* were to me the most wonderful moments that, as a boy, I experienced in the classroom.

"Of Man's first disobedience, and the fruit,
Of that forbidden tree whose mortal taste,
Brought death into the world, and all our woe…"

His clear voice, the resonance of the words he spoke, emphasising the stress measurement of the pentameter, stimulated our interest and captivated our attention. He was able to make his lessons not only enjoyable but also inspirational. It seemed to be important to him that at least some of his students should specialise in English at university and therefore towards the end of our 'A' level course, he sometimes commented that we should be seriously thinking of following a degree course in the 'Queen of Subjects' which for him, of course, was the study of English Literature.

Mrs Evans and Mr Ward were magnificent teachers who passed on to me and other students their love of literature and their sense of fairness and justice. They were ideal models for hard work and decent attitudes. It's true what they say, that a person never forgets a good teacher.

In class, I read whatever I could get my hands on. Greek myths and legends were amongst my favourites. Odysseus resurfaced, blinding Polyphemos and escaping from the cave. This legend from Homer's *The Odyssey* stayed with me and seemed to symbolise the struggle of the immigrant child trying to make sense of his new world, or the adult who faced challenging circumstances. At secondary school, I studied *The Odyssey* for my GCE in Greek Literature. Later, I re-read chapters from *The Odyssey* while studying *Ulysses* by James Joyce at University. The story continued to re-appear at different points in my life and what is Homer's tale if not of a character who, through fate and fortune, finds himself far from home and who is away for so long that home has inevitably changed beyond all recognition but whose memory of home, nevertheless, still pricks his heart with nostalgia. It was like our own predicament, home became a distant romantic dream, a yearning that was not related to our everyday new-found life. In his poem *Ithaka*, CP Cavafy explores this theme of the refugee away from home and the expectation of the return:

As you set out for Ithaka,
hope that your road is a long,
full of adventure, full of discovery.
Laistrygonians, Cyclops,
Angry Poseidon – don't be afraid of them:
you'll never find things like that on your way,
as long as you keep your thoughts raised high,
as long as a rare excitement,
stirs your spirit and your body.
Laistrygonians, Cyclops,
wild Poseidon – you won't encounter them,

unless you bring them along inside your soul,
unless your soul sets them up in front of you.

Hope your road is a long one.
May there be many summer mornings when,
With what pleasure, what joy,
you enter harbours you're seeing for the first time,
may you stop at Phoenician trading stations
to buy fine things,
mother of pearl and coral, amber and ebony,
sensual perfume of every kind,
as many sensual perfumes as you can,
and may you visit many Egyptian cities
to learn and go on learning from their scholars.

Keep Ithaka always in your mind.
Arriving there is what you're destined for.
But don't hurry the journey at all.
Better if it endures for years,
so you're old by the time you reach the island,
wealthy with all you've gained on the way,
not expecting Ithaka to make you rich.[1]

This poem made me feel that we all journey from Ithaka. We all have dangerous encounters with Laistrygonians or Cyclopes. We mostly overcome them and continue our quest for Ithaka. But Ithaka is not a geographical place that you can return to. Laistrygonians can be racist teachers who role up your sleeve and smack your hand until it painfully stings, and Cyclops can be nasty old men who might spit out some racist venom at you in the street. The poem is about present threats and challenges that the individual might be faced with and how the individual must conquer these fearful, negative forces and calmly journey to his or her destination, where ever that may be. It is the spiritual fulfilment and understanding that the earth is the earth, whether you are in Cyprus, England or Ithaka.

I read through the poems of the bilingual text. I read the poems in Greek and often referred to the English translation to make sense of some of the words that I could not understand in Greek. On reflection, the bilingual text represents me and others like me from a different culture and ethnicity who came here or were born here in England and who are both British and something else. This something else, developed and used correctly can only enrich the tapestry of British cultural life, making it colourful and complex.

Rupert the Bear, Peter Rabbit, The Beano, The Beazer and *The Valiant* were the springboards of my reading. By the time I was twelve, I was fluent in reading English. Suddenly, I could read comics and books, newspapers and magazines. I was able to find out about the present and about the past. Inevitably, this led me to read and research about the sad history of the oppressed people of Cyprus and their desire for freedom and peace.

~

The Times and *The Guardian* became favourite newspapers because they contained so much serious reporting of British and foreign news. By the time I had entered the sixth form at Highbury Grove School, I was quite addicted to the reading of broadsheets and showed a critical awareness and response to much that was presented in them. Parallel to this, I was by now reading from the canon of English Literature; *Pygmalion* by George Bernard Shaw, '*Macbeth*', *Othello, The Tempest, A Midsummer Night's Dream* by William Shakespeare, *1984, Brave New World The Portrait of the Artist*, Chaucer, Milton, Dickens, Blake, Wordsworth, Coleridge, the Brontes and so on. The impact on me was enormous. These are only some of the books and authors that have changed my life because they taught me to think not only from a literary point of view but to also consider ethics and morality, justice and injustice, right and wrong. They helped me to give form and shape to my values as a person. In addition, having some brilliant teachers of English like the silver-haired, smiling , talented Mr Ward who could recite chunks from Shakespeare or Chaucer and bring to life the texts, or the enthusiastic kind, generous and caring Mrs Evans, who would decontextualise and put everything into perspective, passed on their love of the subject, and though by now, I am certain that they are no longer with us for they were old when I was no more than a teenager, their love for literature also certainly lives in me and in other former students who had passed through their classrooms.

How does one repay such people, who give that which is good and worthwhile in life to the younger generation, so that goodness spreads out benevolently from one person to the next? It is with their prompting and encouragement that I began to understand the importance of passing my exams and gaining a place at university. They encouraged me with their serious words and friendly gestures, their kind feelings and their belief that I could achieve my goals.

When once, in conversation with Mr Ward, I informed him that I wanted to become a teacher of English, he beamed with a smile and graciously commented,

"The profession needs good teachers and, Fotis, if my hunch is right, you will be a very good teacher."

At these kind words from a teacher who I sincerely respected and deeply admired, I felt both pride and humility at the same time. For my part, I tried to do my best not only for my own benefit but also because I would have felt a terrible embarrassment to have failed the people who had put such faith in me. Mrs Evens' and Mr Ward's kind and caring attitude, their ability to motivate and teach us, their students, and to make us believe that we could succeed, when we sometimes felt that we were on mission impossible, inspired me as a boy at school and continue to inspire me even to this very day.

1. A Bilingual Collection of Poems by C.P. Cavafy. Translated by Edmund Keeley and Philip Sherrard. Loizou Publications. 1998
2. From *Hurricane Hits England* a poem by Grace Nichols.

The Young...and the Old

As a teenager, I sensed the excitement of being in London. It was my home, the place where I lived, went to school, where my friends lived and where I, as a fifteen or sixteen-year-old, began to explore some of the life that it could offer a young man. The excitement of this city has never ceased to amaze me but even more so, when one spring morning, I decided to travel by tube from Finsbury Park, where we lived, to Leicester Square. I'd heard my friends talking about the West End and I had been very rarely since our first visit with my parents to see it. They sometimes spoke about going to the 'pigeons' by which they meant Trafalgar Square or the Queen's Palace by which they meant Buckingham Palace.

This was a time when I had begun to attempt to dress fashionably and to have a trendy teenage appearance. I wore flare jeans and had grown my hair in the style of the Rolling Stones. And one day, feeling rather 'with it', my friends and I decided to catch the tube and head for the West End. On this occasion and countless other times, we walked along Oxford Street gazing in to the shop windows. There were thousands of people crowding the pavements. Somehow, it seemed and felt very different from my first visit some years before when we had gone there with my mother, father and sister to see the Christmas lights. Loud music could be heard from shops, bistros and restaurants. There was the general feeling that this was the beginning of something new and exciting in fashion, music, dance and in the attitude of people to past conventions. The young felt that *The times they are a changing*[1] and as previous younger generations had done before us, we felt that the exciting new future belonged to us. It was without a doubt, the beginning of new kind of cultural revolution that was expressed significantly in the popular music of the period by Bob Dylan, The Beatles, Hendrix and others. There was also a powerful representation of the times in the art of Andy Warhol with his famous portraits of such personalities as Marilyn Monroe, Elizabeth Taylor and Elvis Presley. Another popular artist who captured the mood of the time was Roy Lichtenstein whose paintings were composed of dots and were in the style of comic books that were extremely popular during the sixties and beyond. For those of us who were in our teens, there seemed to be so much going on to inspire our imaginations. We were dazzled by the 'happenings' that brought together psychedelic music, film projection and dance, all going on at the same time. I began to collect music albums by various artists. My hair was long; I wore yellow-tinted glasses in the style of John Lennon and tried to dress in keeping with the psychedelic style. In fact, it was a great time in my life when I'd also completed my 'A' level GCEs and was planning on going to university. While all this was going on, I'd hardly noticed that the smoking of cannabis was becoming more and more popular, particularly at the 'happenings'. LSD also reared its ugly head and was associated closely with the psychedelic movement. People at that time just did not realise that the use of illicit drugs by the very few, who probably had little idea of what they were doing, would eventually lead to the drug taking epidemic that has developed since that time. From hindsight, it is easy to see how terribly naive we all were, but I suppose that is true of every generation who, in the course of time, looks back at its experiences.

I continued to be fascinated by what was going on, particularly in London. I was like a sponge absorbing the excitement of that time. I bought my first record and my taste in music began to develop. I dressed like other teenagers, enjoyed the discos and the parties.

Alongside this cultural development, I took my studies seriously. I aspired to get a place at university. My teachers were friendly and encouraging. I went on school visits to the theatre and saw my first Shakespeare performance at the Old Vic. It was a memorable production of *The Tempest* in which Prospero and his daughter Miranda are exiled from their home and find themselves in difficult circumstances on an island on which they have to make a new life. This was like the experience of my family who also had to make a new beginning in a strange place. I had also begun to appreciate serious films and London must have been then, as it is today, the film capital of the world. There were cinemas everywhere, showing a diversity of films, catering for all tastes. My cultural life was undergoing a sea change and what is surprising is how I felt completely natural at the transformation. At no point did I feel that I was discovering a foreign culture or that I did not belong to this environment. I felt completely that London is where I belonged and that it was absolutely natural for me to enjoy the music of the Beatles, the sound of the Rolling Stones, the lyrics of Bob Dylan, to read the plays of Shakespeare or the poetry of William Wordsworth but at the same time, I also felt very natural and normal with my Greek Cypriot home life. This was, and continues to be, the great attraction about living in London. It is that it allows you, without any hesitation, to be who you are; it allows you to be free and to express yourself and to reveal and be proud of your own uniqueness.

It seems that our sense of Britishness had started to emerge. There was no conscious recognition of this; the change was gradual, in fact, it had started almost from the moment we set foot in the United Kingdom, but now it could be identified more distinctly in the bilingualism and the biculturalism of the young Cypriots who had grown up in London.

At home, we continued to speak Greek because my parents never really learnt English well enough to be able to communicate with it in an uninhibited way. We ate traditional Cypriot food which was, of course, delicious. All our friends and visitors to our home were other Cypriots. We visited their homes and we spoke about Cyprus or about who was getting married to whom within our community. The high point of the week was Sunday. There was always something happening. Often there was a wedding party, or we would have an invitation for dinner, usually from friends who hailed from our village in Cyprus or from some relative who had made the journey to England. Sometimes, there would be guests at our house where Mother and Father welcomed them with traditional Cypriot hospitality. Whatever the occasion, dinner was always a feast. There was *koubebeia* or what some people call dolmades, rice mixed with mincemeat, sprinkled with herbs wrapped in vine leaves like little parcels and cooked in a watery tomato sauce. My favourite dish was *kolokassi yiahni*, or Taro as it is called in English, cooked with chicken in a tomato sauce, sprinkled with fresh lemon. With the delicious dinner, there was usually a bottle of Johnny Walker, Red Label. Seated around the table, eating and drinking, the talk would ensue. The topics were usually predictable: whose son or daughter was getting engaged or married, the birth of children and the latest developments in the never-ending saga of the Cyprus problem. As a boy, I would sit and listen to the conversation of the adults. I observed their habits and internalised their wonderful way of speaking in the Greek Cypriot dialect. I felt even then that I belonged to two worlds and that I could easily slip from one into the other. My parent's world still remained that of their village in Cyprus. Yes, they were now in London, but their only sense of London was their journey to work and back. The only time that they made some kind of contact with English people was when they caught the bus or went to the market. This is when they had the opportunity to use the very little English that they had managed to acquire. "One shilling, Kentish Town, please" or "Six pence, Angel, please." They knew how to ask for their correct fair on the bus simply because it was vital to be able to get around. Another activity that was also important and had to be managed in English was buying food. "One pound apples, please" or "Two pound tomatoes, please." The language was straight forward but it was enough for their simple needs. Sadly, like my parents, most of the ordinary Cypriots who were brave enough to make the journey to what was a distant land for a better life hardly moved beyond that basic level of communicating in English. For them, the most meaningful and satisfying experience was within their own community and within their homes. They spoke their own language and held on to their values and way of life. No real change ever occurred to them. The influence of the new land that they had come to was very marginal and this did not change with time. They remained socially and psychologically in their village. The only change was geography. They actually lived in London. They were like plants that could not thrive in new soil; they could not grow and develop but they did survive and very significantly made it possible for the young to move forward, to take root and to blossom in the new landscape. It was a different reality for those like myself who came to England as children or who had been born here.

1. *The times they are a changing.* Bob Dylan song. Released 1964.

The Old Dialect and the New Language

Time, experience and geography are catalysts for change. It may be that for my parents and their generation who had made the decision to leave their home land and to make a new life in England, ironically for them, who had dared to undertake such an adventure, change remained minimal. They came from a society that was highly traditional and conservative. They felt no need to change and apart from that, the new society into which they had arrived had strong social boundaries that made it difficult for the older generation of immigrants to join. So, they became a community within a community, living and co-existing side by side amongst millions of English people. At that time, perhaps this co-existence was enough, for it was a time when Cypriots and other immigrants to England were settling down and finding their way in a complex North European industrial society. They had come to work and make a better life for their children. They were unconcerned about their social status. That would come later and it would be the mission of the second or third generation of Cypriots in England. Our parents were happy that they had made the journey across the sea to a new land; they were happy that they had work; they were happy that their children had prospects and hope for their future. They were confident that the lives of their children would be better in England than in the land that they had left behind.

For those of us who arrived in England as babies or young children and for those who in due course were born here, it was never going to be sufficient to be a member of a community within a community. England, with its rich language, culture and way of life was irresistibly waiting to absorb the newcomers, but not all could be absorbed. The older generation stuck to its own language and traditions but for the young, it would be a different story.

~

We would go to our church, to Greek weekend schools, mix socially with other Cypriots and to all intents and purposes, gave respect to our parents' aspirations for us. We attended English state schools, became increasingly fluent in spoken English to the point where in due course, English became our main language rather than Greek but we still continued to persevere in speaking Greek in the Cypriot dialect. This gave us a sense of identity and reminded us of our homeland. We felt that if we were to suddenly return to Cyprus, we would fit in without any problems and that our language would be just like everybody else. But many people in Cyprus felt that Cypriots should be closer to Greece and this also meant speaking like our cousins on the mainland. I was as yet unaware of this new trend in how Cypriots should speak their own language. Up to that moment in time, I was quite happy and comfortable speaking in my Cypriot dialect that I had learnt in Sotira and Stylloi as a little child and also because I knew no other way of speaking Greek. I was comfortable and relaxed about how I spoke, that is until we were visited by a friend from Cyprus. Our visitor was a young man named Bambos Kitsis who regarded himself as a person with modern ideas, modern attitudes and a modern way of speaking Greek. So, when I greeted him in the Cypriot dialect and in an uninhibited manner, which in fact was full of warmth and hospitality, his reaction was rather terse.

"Oh," he said, "you speak like a villager. We don't speak like that in Cyprus anymore. Maybe some old people still do but not the younger generation."

I was a little surprised at his reaction and I felt uncertain about what I should do next. I tried to retain my composure and continued to speak Greek to him because he knew no English. At the same time, I became conscious of how I was speaking Greek. I felt that his comments were an attack on my identity because what is the language that one speaks if it is not what one is? In time, it became generally understood by Cypriots that dialect is an enrichment of any language and it should be nurtured and preserved. Unfortunately, people only realise the value of what they have when they are in danger of losing it and sometimes circumstances, historical and social developments change the things that one wants to preserve. Eventually, I came to understand that my unpleasant encounter with Bambos Kistsis illustrated the illogical beliefs that Cypriots had been taught that their Cypriot Greek or Cypriot Turkish languages were not quite right and were better replaced by the standard languages of the 'motherlands'.

~

Most Cypriot teenagers who had grown up in London joined the teenage revolution. We dressed like our favourite pop singers, we listened to the music of the popular bands of the time and we showed our enthusiasm to succeed socially and educationally. Most of us were becoming very British in language, style, culture and outlook and we were liking it. There may have been some confusing attitudes about how young London Cypriots spoke Greek but there was no confusion about how well we had acquired the English language and how much we were beginning to enjoy living in London.

While young Cypriots were adopting the British popular culture of the time, there was also a feeling of change in Cyprus. Despite the political problems of the island, tourism was beginning to take off. People were beginning to enjoy a higher standard of living and had a lot more money in their pockets. Tourism began to change the narrow, blinkered mentality of Cypriots and this was reflected in their life styles and attitude. This happened not suddenly but over a period of years. Change wasn't immediately apparent, but it was obvious enough to be noticed by Cypriots from England returning to Cyprus during the late sixties and certainly prior to 1974 and to also comment on how Cyprus had changed and how people were now different – less welcoming, less generous.

Many Cypriots had also begun to use standard Greek in their everyday lives. The influence of television and the wider access to secondary and higher education led to people speaking in what they thought to be a more educated or sophisticated Greek instead of the traditional dialect of Cyprus. In London, Cypriots, however, continued to speak the Cypriot dialect that their parents had brought with them during the 1950s and 1960s before the shift from dialect to standard Greek had begun to take hold amongst the general population of Cyprus. I personally feel that it is rather sad that Cypriots have embraced the evolution from dialect to standard form with such enthusiasm without due regard for a form of Greek that according to legend, was brought to Cyprus by Agapenor, an Arcadian, and his followers who on their return voyage from Troy, were carried by the winds to Cyprus where they founded the city of Paphos. It must be said that the Greek Cypriot dialect is immensely rich in traditional stories and folk songs and has contributed greatly to the variety and richness of the Greek language. I can only conjuncture that the psychological reason for the willingness of Cypriots to accept such drastic changes in their expression of the Greek language was not only the inevitable influence of the mass media but also because of their age-old insecurity of their status as true Hellenes. Perhaps, they felt that if you speak like the Athenians, you can somehow be more Hellenic. There was no clear thinking on this important issue.

From another point of view, could anyone expect that while the world changed, people in Cyprus should remain static and unchanging? Older

Cypriots from England noticed the change more starkly simply because their attitude and cultural outlook remained trapped in the 1950s. Being in England meant that they could not develop in the same way as other people in the country because of their lack of the English language and neither could they be a part of the cultural changes that were beginning to evolve in Cypriot society because they were so far away. To complicate matters further, young Cypriots in England who had grown up with the strong influence of British culture could not help beginning to forge their identity within the context of their present and immediate environment. There were uncertainties that had to be confronted. If you had been born in England or if you had come to England as a little child and you spoke mainly English, what were you? If you had never been to Cyprus or if most of your experience had been in England, where should you feel that you belonged? Who were your people? What was your identity? These feelings became even more poignant when young Cypriots visited Cyprus and discovered that they spoke in dialect form that was no longer popular with the young people of Cyprus, who were now attempting to use the standard form of Greek and would sometimes unkindly comment that their Cypriot relatives from England spoke in an uneducated manner. Needless to say, British Cypriots felt that such comments were inconsiderate and showed a lack of sensitivity. But to be absolutely fair, we know that features of language are constantly changing and these often depend on social, political, economic and geographical factors. This is what happened to language in Cyprus as it also happens everywhere else with other languages and we can see, as an example of this, how English has changed in the past fifty years. But my spoken Greek is in the form of the Cypriot dialect that my parents spoke when we came to England in the fifties. Being cut off from Cyprus, our Greek Cypriot dialect (in London) developed its own unique features, a mixture of Greek Cypriot syntax and English vocabulary! The development of language in Cyprus evolved in its own particular way and it will be interesting to see how the influx of thousands of people from Russia will impact upon it. One thing is easily noticed and that is the Greek Cypriot dialect of British Cypriots is now different in comparison to how people speak in Cyprus. We can see now with some clarity that geographical journeys change the migrant community and its members in an economic and social manner so that it gradually, over a period of years, adopts and acquires the manners, habits and beliefs of the people it has joined. Are British Cypriots now more British and less Cypriot? My belief is that they are increasingly so, and that is as it should be because how else can you live your life unless it is to engage fully within your immediate environment and play a full and significant part within the society in which live? We might further add that we are all very fortunate that the United Kingdom is a democratic country that has encouraged the ethnic minorities to develop in accordance with the vision that they have of themselves.

Nationality

We now have clearer concepts of British nationality and a variety of labels that identify the different ethnic groups that have come to England or have evolved here, but this all came later as a response to the new circumstances that emerged with the arrival of millions of new comers to these shores. The people of my generation who came here as children from Cyprus were commonly identified as Cypriot or Greek, but the label confused the reality. By the time that I was a teenager, I could hardly remember Cyprus and had never been to Greece. The truth is that people like myself were British because we were here and knew no other way of life, had almost no experience other than of England. It was rather uncomfortable to be constantly reminded about being Greek by our parents or by the well-intentioned school teachers who wanted to celebrate multiculturalism and who assumed that we were somehow experts about the life of people in Cyprus or Greece. There were a few clear-thinking people who were able to clarify some of the confusion felt by young Cypriots in search of an identity that they could really accept and say 'yes, that is us'. One such wise individual was Mr Griffin, a teacher at my school. He was at least six feet tall, slim, his blond hair was thinning, and he had bright, piercing blue eyes. He smoked a pipe and every time you saw him in school, he had a mug of tea in his hand. He had been in the RAF during the war and had become an emergency trained teacher after its conclusion. He was a history teacher and had the ability to inspire his students through discussion and the telling of stories about the war based on his real-life experiences. His stories were full of adventure and suspense. They were about Spitfires being scrambled for action above the skies of the home counties during The Battle of Britain or Lancaster bombers on missions over Nazi Germany. He had been there, he was a part of it and the boys in his charge knew this and listened intently to his recollections of the greatest war in the history of mankind.

On one occasion, however, we got onto a totally different subject, the subject of nationality. He asked the group,

"What nationality do you think that you are?"

"I'm British," said my friend Michael.

"I'm Scottish and you'd better not call me British," said another boy.

We all laughed and then Mr Griffin turned to me.

"What nationality are you, Fotis?"

"I'm Greek," I answered instinctively.

Mr Griffin paused, lowered his tone, spoke kindly, trying to clarify matters.

"No, Fotis. Your nationality is British."

I was surprised by this announcement in front of the class. Mr Griffin paused and I waited, looking intensely at him. I had always been Greek to everyone around me so what did he mean by this?

"Your nationality, Fotis, is British. You have a Greek ethnicity and you were born in Cyprus, you can speak Greek, your religion is Greek Orthodox, but your nationality is British."

I didn't quite understand what the difference was between nationality and ethnicity but Mr Griffin, in his calm, cool and clear manner made me realise that I did not just belong to my Greek Cypriot past but also to my British present.

"When you were born in Cyprus and even when your mother and father were born there, you were of Greek Cypriot ethnicity, but your nationality was British because Cyprus, your place of birth, was a British colony, a part of the British Empire."

I looked into Mr Griffin's piercing blue eyes and tried to understand what he was saying. He had spoken without malice and with a genuine need to correct assumptions that needed to be addressed. In time, I realised that what Mr Griffin had been trying to explain was the reality based on historical facts.

~

The question of identity has remained to this day, a source of confusion for both Greek Cypriots and Turkish Cypriots. Many Cypriots who have been born and raised in England will say that we are Greek/Turkish and not Greek/Turkish Cypriot. We hardly ever state that we are British. I believe that this is said unthinkingly and doesn't do justice to our experience in England. It may be that when we say that we are Greek or Turkish, we are merely stating our historical background, but this is inaccurate because we are not from Greece or Turkey. More accurately, in order to describe our background and our present identity, we should use the term British Cypriot, which I think is accurate and can be used by Cypriots of all backgrounds without political controversy.

~

In Cyprus, it is just as confusing. Greek flags are shown in the south while Turkish flags are shown in the north. In contrast to the voices of propaganda, inaccurate history and religion in recent years, science has attempted to bring some truth to the confusion of ethnicity in Cyprus. The DNA testing of the population, both Greek and Turkish Cypriot has revealed that the makeup of the Cypriots is diverse and rather mixed. While containing elements from the two so-called motherlands, the results also show that Greek and Turkish Cypriot DNA contains a mixture of elements from all the surrounding countries that at one time or another, have occupied the island of Cyprus. A further interesting and ironic twist in the story of Cypriot DNA is that it links the Turkish Cypriots with the DNA of people from Northern Greece and in particular, Thessaloniki. The explanation for this is that the people who migrated from central Asia Minor to Cyprus during the Ottoman era were related to the Christian refugees who fled from Asia Minor during the Greco-Turkish War of 1919–1921. It is plain and simple, our Turkish Cypriot fellow countrymen are related to our cousins in Greece while the Greek Cypriots are related to our neighbours and cousins of the Turkish Cypriots, the Turks! For the incurable, fanatical nationalists of both sides, who imagine that they are the direct descendants of Leonidas and his Spartans or of Attila the Hun and his marauding, conquering army, the DNA revelation is a slap in the face – that is if they have the capability to understand the historical and political significance of what science has shown to us. It would be very sad if Cypriots did not interpret the findings in a manner that would bring the two communities together and not to remain so uncertain, confused and bewildered about their own identity. After all, the evidence indicates very clearly the people of Cyprus are indeed, nothing more or nothing less than *Kuprioi* or *Kibrislilar*. Knowing who you really are and being able to come to terms with the truth is always better than believing in some mythical stories that are unreal and that have been used as propaganda to brain wash us into believing them.

~

Those of us who had grown up in London had our own issues of identity that needed to be addressed. We felt the stress of belonging in two camps and when amongst our own families and relatives, we expressed our ethnicity through language, music or dance, attending on occasion the Greek Orthodox Church; it was a different matter when we were with friends at school, shopping in Oxford Street or on a night out at a disco. At such times, there would occur an ethnic metamorphosis into a Britishness exhibited in fashion, taste in music and amongst other features

175

of the transformation was the fluency in English. These perceptions of identity, these experiments in the presentation of ourselves happened quite naturally and without any preconceived ideas about who we were and what we were trying to become. The process was instinctive and, I suppose, inevitable and sometimes it was in stark opposition to the aspirations and wishes of our parents who persevered in teaching us our ethnic language when it had become easier and of more benefit to use English both at home and other places.

Arrangement or Romance?

An issue that caused a great deal of tension between young Cypriots who had grown and reached maturity in London and their parents was the choice of marriage partner. The parents almost always wanted their boys to marry Cypriot girls, to speak Greek and to dress smartly but in a conventional manner. Nobody asked the Cypriot girls what they wanted; it was assumed that they would quietly do the bidding of their parents, who in general, mocked what they considered to be the extremes of fashion like long hair or flamboyant clothes for boys or miniskirts and heavy make up for girls. I'm afraid to say that my parents were very disappointed when as a sixth former, I grew my hair like many of my school friends and began to dress in flared jeans and floral shirts. My father's teasing had a serious edge to it as he would sometimes comment, "Fotaki, with your long hair you look like a girl. Go and have a haircut and dress like a man."

This was rather unfair because I was only being like other people of my age. Somehow, the older generation of Cypriots could not quite understand that coming to England also meant that in due course, we would do things more like the English. How would it be possible to remain unchanged or unaffected by those with whom we now shared the same geographical location. Apart from this, fashion was becoming international so what Cypriot parents despised in London fashions was also being copied by the young in Cyprus.

Sometimes, we were visited by my sister who was already married and on occasion, she was accompanied by her mother and father-in-law. Their names were Koumis and Maria. They were both elderly, typical Cypriot village people who had very strong Christian values who, in most respects, were full of humour and kindness, but they were utterly intolerant of anyone who had a different view of the world from themselves. Hence, when they visited our house and saw me with my long hair and colourful shirt, I immediately became the focus of their attention and the target of their negative remarks.

"You have become like a goat with your hair so long," they would say and look away from me and continue to address my mother, who often found their company unpleasant.

"You know these long-haired people, they are all hashish smokers and you can't trust them."

"My Foti would never do a thing like that, he is far too sensible. He only has long hair because it is the fashion amongst the young people."

My sister's in-laws seemed unconvinced and continued to look at me as if I had just arrived from another planet. My mother always sprung to my defence and after their visit she commented with a smile on her face,

"They really are such thick-headed villagers."

After one or two such experiences with my sister's in-laws, I quickly vacated the house if I heard that there was an impending visit. Many years after, when on holiday in Cyprus, we happened to be in Avgorou from where Koumis and Maria had come from and where they had returned to live. We visited them, and they welcomed us with utter warmth. Unexpectedly, just as we were about to get into the car to leave, the now very elderly Maria looked at me and in a very serious manner said,

"I am so glad, Foti, that you have cut that horrible long hair. Now you smell like a real man."

I thanked her for her hospitality, a little surprised that the issue of boys growing their hair long in keeping with the fashion of the time had been so significant for her.

~

The Cypriot parents who made the journey to England as adults and whose children were either born or were raised in England did not think that their children would be different from them. They imagined that the new generation would be as Cypriot as they were, but alas, how could this be? The parents were to be disappointed in their expectations and one of the issues that clearly pointed to the difference between the older generation and their anglicised children was the tradition of the arranged marriage. For the parents, it was unthinkable that their children should not go through the process of the traditional arranged marriage. There was certainly much friction in families regarding this matter, but eventually it was the parents who lost the battle and surrendered to the inevitable. Their children eventually broke this particular tradition and claimed their right to have the choice about who they married. Cypriots adopted the 'romantic' relationship as a means to choosing their marriage partner and, of course, we all know that romance does not recognise differences in colour, race or creed. Cypriots of both sexes began to marry outside of the community and though at first this seemed rather uncomfortable, over a span of a few years it had become quite normal. The success in breaking out of the ethnic cocoon and recognising that you cannot live in a narrow existence imported from elsewhere is an important step in the development of ethnic communities, living either here or elsewhere in the world.

For the Cypriot community, it has not meant that it is less Cypriot; it merely showed that we were also more British and beginning to feel more comfortable with our new environment and the new way of life.

Enoch

In the late 1960s, the idea of multiculturalism gathered pace. Its intention was to celebrate diversity in British society and to teach particularly children to respect each other's language, culture, religion and way of life. It was felt by liberal minded people that there was a need for British society to change and to educate itself in response to the new social conditions of a population that almost overnight had changed in composition and would continue to do so in the years ahead. This was an appropriate response to right wing populist politicians who gambled on furthering their careers by playing the race card.

One such political figure was Enoch Powel[1] who said that the British were 'mad' to accept so many alien people into these islands and prophesised that there would be 'Rivers of blood' implying that there would be some kind of apocalyptic conflict between the British people and the new arrivals. 'The Rivers of Blood' speech[2] was Enoch Powell's response to increasing immigration to this country and to the anti-discrimination laws that had been introduced. Interestingly, it is likely that this speech by Powell, who was an MP for the Conservative Party in opposition, is thought to have contributed to the surprise Conservative Party general election victory of 1970 which brought Edward Heath to power. From this result, we can see many British people may indeed have been sympathetic to Enoch Powell's view on immigration.

The speech itself was directed at 'the ordinary Englishman'. Its purpose was to warn him of the consequences of large scale immigration to this country. It presented the immigrants as people who would take over the land, pushing the English population to one side. The speech had the obvious intention of instilling fear and panic into ordinary citizens. It was also intended to provoke action in order to prevent the supposed takeover of the land by alien people. Here is an extract from the speech:

"We must be mad as a nation to be permitting the annual inflow of some 50,000 dependents who, for the most part, are material for the future growth of the immigrant descendent population. It is like watching a nation busily engaged in heaping up its own funeral pyre. So insane are we that we actually permit unmarried persons to immigrate for the purpose of founding a family with spouses and fiancées who they have never seen."

In an opinion poll taken by the Gallup Poll Organisation[3] shortly after the speech, it was found that 74% of people questioned agreed with the views expressed in Enoch Powell's speech.

Father couldn't help picking up bits of information about what was going on. He detested Edward Heath because he was the Conservative Prime Minister and in my father's eyes, the leader of the wealthy classes who didn't much care for the problems of working class people and in particular, the problems of immigrants like ourselves. But Father also understood that politicians like Edward Heath and Harold Wilson, the leader of the Labour Party and whom my father greatly admired, were very different from this Enoch Powell who was hardly noticed before his racist and inflammatory speech. His 'Rivers of blood' speech was shown on the television news with what appeared to be large scale support from the public. When my father saw this, he became rather worried and anxiously questioned me about it.

"What is he saying about us?" asked my father.

I didn't quite understand Enoch Powell's use of imagery.

"I think he is saying that the river is going to be full of blood and he keeps talking about immigrants."

I did my best to translate what the speech was about.

"What else is he saying?" Father persisted.

"I think he is saying that there are too many immigrants here in England and soon, there will not be any place for English people to live. I think he is saying that we should all get out of England."

My father had comprehended enough; he then exploded with outrage and anger.

"Who does he think he is, this terrible man? He is like another Hitler! He is using racism to frighten the English people so that he can become a popular politician and gain power. This man is a scoundrel who is prepared to see bloodshed on the streets just to further his ambitions. The Labour Party will never allow this to happen!"

I looked at Father in amazement; he was speaking about Hitler, racism, the Labour Party and the Conservative Party. He seemed so informed, he knew what was going on and could even interpret the speech of a British politician on the basis of my very simplistic translation into Greek. This was one of those moments when I felt proud of him.

Father had faith that good would triumph over evil and in this case, good was represented by the Labour Party who would deal with the incredibly unscrupulous Enoch Powell. Mother, however, was not as confident that this problem would be dealt with by what my father called people of goodwill.

"Loizo, these people do not want us here in their country."

She spoke quietly and with a perplexed expression on her face.

"Can't you see," she continued, "that many of them look at us with contempt, make comments at us in the streets. Now they are marching with flags and banners. They have a leader and they are following him. Are you sure that we and our children are safe here?"

After Mother had spoken for a few minutes, there was a silence in the room as if we were all taking in the significance of the moment.

"We will be alright," my father broke in reassuringly.

Mother was unconvinced. For her, this really was a time of uncertainty and she often talked about returning to Cyprus despite the problems that she would find there.

~

The British liberal establishment kicked back by launching multiculturalism to run as a major theme in education and in the defining policies of all public British institutions. This was the powerful response of the liberal establishment to the evil of racism and for the most immediate needs, it certainly worked. The school curriculum was revised to reflect Britain as a multicultural society. Black culture and black history were introduced, as was the study of world religions. Black and Asian people became a common phenomenon on television and in areas of responsibility. I am not saying that all problems based on race disappeared over night or that as a result of multiculturalism, we had succeeded in transforming Britain into some kind of utopia that was devoid of racism and prejudice. But without a doubt, multiculturalism improved the understanding that people of different races living in this country had of each other. But all this had yet to be achieved. It certainly didn't happen overnight

Meanwhile, Enoch Powell's speech had created immediate tension on the streets. There were almost instant demonstrations by the dock workers who, on the 23rd of April, 1970, went on strike, marching to the Palace of Westminster to protest against the sacking of Powell from the cabinet by Edward Heath. They carried placards that declared 'Back Britain, not Black Britain'. Leading political figures on the whole condemned the speech as inflammatory and damaging to race relations. But Enoch Powell was not without support amongst the political elite. Margaret Thatcher, an important member of the government and future prime minister, called his speech 'strong meat', expressing reluctance to support actions against him.

~

As a result of the Powell's speech, there was an increase in racist abuse in the streets. Sometimes, my parents came home from work and exclaimed their outrage at having been called 'bloody foreigners' or when they were rudely told to 'go back to where you come from'. The xenophobia that had been deliberately unleashed by this opportunist demagogue also extended into the school where English school children adopting and learning the attitudes of their parents and elders began a bullying campaign against immigrant children. Cypriot children were victimised and called names: 'Greek bubbles' or 'Greek bastards'. The same epithets were used against our Turkish Cypriot fellow students because for the English racists, we were just the same! Some English students formed into gangs and attacked us or other ethnic minority children for no other reason than for being of a different colour or race. We often moved around the school in real fear of attack from these young racist thugs. Some immigrant children were so fearful that they refused to go to school. They would set off for school in the morning but never arrived. Instead, they walked around the streets, rode on the tube or went to the cinema.

In huge contrast to the conditions of today in which it is common to find an anti-racist policy in the prospectus and mission statement of any school in the United Kingdom, the teachers at that time just did not know what to do or how to react in response to the monster of racism that had reared its head in their midst. It was to be sometime before educators and teachers would themselves fully understand the problem of racism and introduce effective programmes in the education curriculum to fight ingrained racist attitudes.

Luckily, the direct hostility engendered by Powell's speech and Powellism did not overtly endure and people, with the passing of time, were able to address the problems presented by a society in a state of flux. My father, after all, was right. People of goodwill did not allow Enoch Powell and his racist followers to succeed. In time, though even now it has not entirely disappeared, most of the racist verbal abuse on the streets faded away. The teddy boy and later the skinhead hostility and violence towards ethnic minorities was never very wide spread and it also came to an end. Without a doubt, education had a great deal to do with combating racism in the United Kingdom but more than this, it was the common sense, the moderate attitude and the sense of fair play of the majority of people in the United Kingdom that enabled a multicultural society to evolve.

1. Enoch Powell was a man of notable achievements. He had been awarded the MBE and had graduated in Classics from Oxford University. He had also been an accomplished philologist, poet and writer. His speeches, before the 'Rivers of Blood' episode, were sagacious and enriched by memorable sayings: "History is littered with wars that everybody knew would never happen."
"If my ship sails from sight, it doesn't mean my journey ends, it simply means my river bends."
He was Minister for Health under the Premiership of Edward Heath and was thought to have been an obvious and strong contender for the leadership of the Conservative Party when the opportunity would arise. Wikipedia.
Are we therefore not surprised and astonished that such an enlightened politician as Enoch Powell would have adopted a populist agenda and to have used racial hatred for the sake of furthering his political career? Fortunately, the spontaneous support that was given to him was not to have any major lasting effect.

2. The 'Rivers of Blood' speech was delivered by Enoch Powell at a Conservative Association Meeting in Birmingham on 20th of April, 1968. Enoch Powell's 'Rivers of Blood' speech, The Telegraph, 6th November, 2006.

3. The Gallup poll asked the general public whether they supported the view expressed by Enoch Powell in his 'Rivers of Blood' speech. "In 1968, a British politician warned immigration would lead to violence. Now some say he was right." World View, Adam Taylor, The Washington Post, 24th November, 2015.

Waiting for the Bus

Not long after the 'Rivers of Blood' speech, I experienced a disturbing incident on the streets of London. I had not long completed my 'A' level GCE examinations and having gone through the rigours of three months of intensive revision followed by some very tough examinations, my fellow students and I were all very keen to put this trying experience behind us and have a good time. It happened that on one particular Saturday night, I had been invited to a party by one of my friends from school whose parents were away for the weekend. He lived in a large Victorian house in Camden Mews, just off Camden Road. I had arrived at about 9 pm and the party was already in full swing. Most of the people present were from the sixth form of Highbury Grove School. Everyone was looking trendy. The girls were in miniskirts and the boys all had long hair with patterned shirts that had unusually big collars. The music was loud and rhythmic. There was a tasty choice: The Rolling Stones sang their greatest hit *Here comes my 19th nervous breakdown*, and The Kinks oozed with London sophistication with *Dedicated follower of fashion* and *Sunny Afternoon*. There were hits by The Animals and lots of music by my favourite, Cat Stevens.

Everyone had brought a bottle or two and some of the guests were already rather merry and dancing in the middle of the living room. Our host, whose name was Andreas, had gone to the trouble of creating a real party atmosphere by setting up multi-coloured lights that flashed while the music blared loudly from the latest stereophonic music centre. The doorbell rang every five minutes. Some people were leaving early while others were only just arriving. There were people everywhere: some were sitting on the staircase, others occupied the corridor. Inside the living room, the lights had been dimmed and couples were dancing with their arms tightly wound around each other. There was laughter and loud talking. The house was full of cigarette smoke but in those days, nobody seemed to care.

I felt relaxed and good about myself because I had completed my 'A' levels and now was the time to celebrate. After a couple of beers, I lit up a cigarette just to look cool in front of some of the girls. When I inhaled,

I thought of how angry Mother would be with me if she saw me with a cigarette in my mouth. I tried to push the thought out of my mind. Eventually, I danced around with some friends for a while and then I had some more beer and was really enjoying myself. It was then that, quite by chance, I happened to look at the little carriage clock on the mantle shelf. When I looked carefully at it, I realised that it was time for me to leave. The time was 12:45 and the last bus along Camden Road would be going by at approximately 1 am.

"Andreas, I've gotta go now, gotta catch the last bus. Great party, see ya later mate!"

Andreas looked up from the pretty girl he was embracing.

"Hey, Foti, why ya going so early for? The party's only just starting."

A friend called out teasingly,

"Mummy will be angry, Foti, if you're not home by the deadline," then they all broke out in loud laughter.

I had already opened the front door to exit before they could continue with their silly jokes. They liked to tease, and I didn't mind because they were my friends. I closed the door behind me and walked down the quiet mews towards the main road.

I felt the cool air drying the perspiration on my forehead. I had had a very good time and it had been a real pleasure to see my friends from school. Walking at a brisk pace while humming to myself the Cat Stevens hit, *I love my dog as much as I love you*, I soon reached the bus stop that was situated outside the gates of the Jewish Free School along Camden Road.

There was another person at the bus stop waiting for the last bus. It was a pretty, young woman, probably the same age as me or even a little younger. She was standing very still and had quite a serious expression on her face. She made no attempt to speak or look in my direction so we both waited quietly, looking in the direction from where we expected the night bus to appear. There was a gentle, warm breeze that made the night feel cool and refreshing. An occasional motor car would go by from time to time. A dog could be heard barking somewhere in the distance. Everything seemed full of peace and tranquillity. The girl and I, now hardly aware of each other, stood at the bus stop, breathing in the cool night air, waiting for the bus.

We had not been long at the bus stop when suddenly there was a loud commotion to be heard coming in our direction. The peace and quiet had suddenly been disturbed. Having turned off from one of the side roads, we could see four young men heading in our direction. They were kicking an empty beer can around and shouted obscene remarks at passing motorists. They laughed in an exaggerated manner and screamed at the top of their

186

voices. The girl and I looked in their direction and then for a moment, feeling alarmed, at each other. There was no one else around except for the four rowdy individuals who were drawing closer and closer to us with every passing second.

When the rowdy gang of four noticed the young woman and me at the bus stop, they suddenly became very quiet. They briefly stopped, looked, said something to each other and then proceeded towards us. I couldn't help feeling that there was going to be a problem. I looked again down the road for any sign of the bus but unfortunately there was no sign of it.

Before long, the gang had reached the bus stop and had strategically placed themselves between me and the girl.

I couldn't help noticing that the members of the gang were dressed in smart jeans and shirts. They didn't look thuggish, but it was obvious that they had been drinking. I was hopeful that nothing unpleasant was going to happen. The young woman looked composed and hadn't panicked by their stares. They remained silent for a couple of minutes while they stared at the girl in a cold manner that must have made her feel very uncomfortable. I stood still and silent, trying to look indifferent and as if nothing was amiss. Then they started.

One of them approached the girl and stood very close to her. He breathed right into her face and looking at her directly in the eyes with a silly smirk, said, "Well, I've seen lots of girls tonight, but you must be the sexiest."

He turned and grinned at his onlookers while they grinned back and egged him on. In his stupidity, he probably felt that the girl found him and his approach irresistible. The girl retained her composure and calmly ignoring him turned to one side, looking out towards the road. Her message was clear that she didn't want to be bothered. His friends and audience burst out laughing at him.

"She ain't interested in you," said one while the other joined in,

"Better luck next time!"

They jeered and laughed at him. The jilted suitor stood there, not knowing how to respond, then one of his friends stepped forward.

"Step aside and look at how it's done by a master."

"Go on, John, whooooah!"

Two of them called out while the failed suitor looked on to see if his friend could do better than him.

His friends continued to snigger at the new would-be suitor because what he had said must have highlighted even to them how foolish he actually sounded. He then approached the girl from behind while she was looking blankly across the road and grabbed her arm, violently swung her round to face him. He tried to grab her by the waist and to kiss her on the lips. In her panic, the girl screamed and struggled against her assailant.

"What ya doin'! Are ya crazy! Leave me alone, will ya! I'll call a cop if ya don't watch out," she threatened hopelessly but at that moment in time, it seemed that all the night buses and all the policemen in the world had suddenly disappeared.

I wasn't surprised by the verbal abuse of these individuals but at that moment I was shocked by the physical attack on the girl. It was time to do something. I knew that I would end up getting a beating because all four of them were big guys, but I just could not help myself.

"Please! Leave her alone! She's frightened!"

My intervention seemed feeble even to me and I was fully aware of the possible consequences. All at once, as if I had rudely reminded them of my existence, they turned and faced me. The girl realising that I was her only protection on the deserted scene ran and stood behind me. She was shocked and frightened. All her detached composure had evaporated as she clutched to the back of my jacket. I could also see that the gang of four were very intoxicated. Their eyes were blood shot and their faces full of hostility because I had dared to intervene in their proceedings. The self-assured one, who had been embarrassed by the girl, came towards me with glaring, red eyes and growled at me through clenched teeth as if his jaw had been stapled together.

"Are ya talkin' to me, ya little Greek bastard! Are ya talkin' to me!" he repeated as if in outraged disbelief. Meanwhile, the other members of the gang began to encircle us like a hunting pack. Their fists were clenched and they were ready to pounce.

I was just saying that you're frightening her…there's no need, but I was the one who was now really frightened.

With this, they became even more infuriated and seemed to be on the verge of a mad assault.

"Who ya tellin' what to do, ya Greek bastard… I'm gonna break your legs before Enoch sends ya home! I'm gonna cripple ya!"

They were building their anger into a frenzy.

The girl and I stood there frightened. We didn't know what to do. We expected the worst. They roared and screamed abuse but there was no attack. Perhaps, they had not as yet developed their true violent potential. Despite my sense of panic and fear at that moment, something that my would-be assailant said, echoed in my mind.

"…before Enoch sends ya home…before Enoch sends ya home…"

"Ya Greek bastard!" another one yelled and pushed me so that I staggered backwards, crashing into the girl who was standing behind me.

The image of the teacher with the thin red lips suddenly and unexpectedly flashed across my mind.

"That will teach you a lesson!" she sneered with her red rouged lips. Then the old man with the bowler hat and an angry face, in an instant rose up before me, holding his umbrella like a cudgel ready to strike me for Queen and Empire:

"Enoch's gonna break your legs, ya Greek bastard!" growled the nasty old man.

The girl's voice suddenly brought me back to my senses.

"Look, the bus is coming!" she exclaimed into my ear while helping me back on to my feet.

Unexpectedly, the late-night bus appeared, as if out of thin air. In the confusion of what was happening, the bus had approached the stop. The driver must have sensed what was going on. It was our chance to make an escape. Instinctively, I grabbed the girl's hand and we both jumped onto the platform of the route master. Before the gang of four, in their drunken stupor could respond, the West Indian bus conductor had rung the bell and the bus drove off, leaving the four thugs stranded on the Camden Road.

"It looks like ya havin' some problem with those guys," said the bus conductor with a Caribbean accent and a friendly smile on his face.

"Na, they were just a bit drunk. Nothing we couldn't handle," I said with a laugh.

I was trying to look cool about the whole matter. But the girl and I both knew that it could have ended very badly for us, we'd had a lucky escape. In the safety and warmth of the bus, we sat together, talking and feeling relieved that we had escaped from those thugs. Just before she got off at Holloway Road, she embraced and kissed me on the cheek.

"Thanks, I was really scared, and you were very brave. See ya around."

She was really stunningly beautiful, and I always hoped that I would run into her somewhere or other but unfortunately it did not happen. I never saw her again. But one thing is for certain, I think that like myself, she will always remember the night when we waited together for the late-night bus.

A happy ending you might think that remained a fond memory but also because eventually, the racist demagogy of Enoch Powel was not bought by the vast majority of the British people and Enoch as a politician very soon sank into oblivion and was only revered by a small number of fanatics who maintained that he had the gift of prophecy.

~

It may have surprised Enoch and his followers, but most people were willing to learn about each other's cultures and traditions and to be enriched by this experience. It was a slow process, an evolvement in the understanding of new circumstances in society. The media was another powerful tool through which white, Anglo-Saxon society was influenced into a more positive way of thinking about people of a different race, colour or creed. There were films like *To Sir with Love* starring Sidney Poitier as a new black teacher, who arrives at a London secondary school and is faced by white students, who are very hostile to him because of his colour. The film is about how the young and naïve students who did not know any better learn that their black teacher is a caring individual who has the talent to help them develop as human beings. They learn how to respect the person and to rid themselves of their racist attitudes. Alongside Sidney Poitier was the very young Lulu who played in the role of one of the young, unruly and prejudiced teenagers that created a headache for their new black teacher. As the plot of the film unfolds, she and her friends learn that people should be judged for their values and not by the colour of their skin. The theme song to the film was also performed by Lulu. It was one of her best songs and remains a haunting reminder of early attempts to tackle the ugliness of racism. I remember going to the cinema with my friends to see this film. At the end of the film, we emerged from the cinema smiling because of the happy ending but also aware and influenced by the film's message of love and respect for each other. There were other films with similar content and message.

Today, we know that in certain respects, this feature of multiculturalism has worked quite well because, on the whole, people stopped noticing that a news presenter like Trevor McDonald is black but rather appreciated his professional delivery of the news to a nationwide audience. This was possible due to the ability of the majority of the people to take on the changes in society and to respond in a fair and balanced manner. This has enabled ethnic minority people to express their talents in a very broad area of national life including business, industry, medicine, the arts, sport, the armed forces and so on. Has British society and culture not benefitted by the influx of people from the Commonwealth and from other parts of the world? People like the late Enoch Powell with his apocalyptic visions of 'Rivers of Blood' and others of his ilk have been proved quite mistaken in their projections because the voice of justice, fairness and moderation, have prevailed. There have been no 'Rivers of Blood'.

The Arranged Marriage

My sister Kika did not achieve her academic potential. Instead, like most young women of her background, while still in her teens, she was faced with an arranged marriage.

The weddings were an outward symbol, they tried to show a community that was well ordered, prosperous and while settling into its new country of abode, it continued to emphasise the importance of its ancient customs and traditions. It seems that life was more straightforward for the young women who had arrived in England in their late teens or in their twenties, who were already adults and who therefore identified more strongly with the way of life of the older generation of Cypriots.

It was not so simple for the girls who had arrived as young children or who were born here in the United Kingdom and attended schools in London or some other British city. These British Cypriots faced the impact of the fashions, styles, the ideas and attitudes of British teenagers who were involved in their own teenage revolution facilitated by increasing wealth and influenced by new ideas and developments in society. The birth control pill[1] had been introduced and became a catalyst for change. It was a sexual revolution that ended the notion of the subservient woman who would go from being a daughter to being a wife. Feminism had re-emerged from its slumber and with a more powerful voice. Perhaps the politician who reflected the spirit of the time was Roy Jenkins[2] in his speech in which he referred to 'the civilised society'. This memorable phrase implied many things including the right of women to belong to themselves and not to any other master as dictated by custom or religion.

These ideas entered the consciousness of young ethnic minority women who had grown up in the United Kingdom, had attended school with British teenagers and had observed them enjoying a life style and freedom that was denied to them. My sister Kika was one such a teenager who had the possibility of living a very different life from that which was planned by our parents. She was, I know, uncomfortable with the idea of an arranged marriage but at the age of seventeen, she did not have the voice to resist parents and the powerful force of tradition. When my sister had hardly turned sixteen, our parents began to introduce the subject of getting engaged.

Sometimes, Mother would utter very softly, "You are sixteen years old already, Kika. Soon a handsome young man from a good family will see you at a wedding party or at the church and then it will be your turn to marry."

Our parents spoke kindly to her about this matter as if they were trying to persuade a child to do something that the child could not really understand.

Then Mother, who was more practical than Father, would add, "Not just someone in tight trousers who will gamble and drink. Such men are a waste of time. Your future husband should have a trade and be a good worker."

As Mother spoke these words to my sister, she looked at her with immense love and pride but there was also a hint of worry in her look and uncertainty in her voice.

Kika wouldn't argue with our parents even if she didn't like what they were saying; she would become very quiet and sullen. I understood that she was unhappy about marrying so young, but she had been brought up to be an obedient girl. In Cypriot tradition, it was demanded that girls should be obedient daughters and then obedient wives. She had never been encouraged to ask questions, to disagree or to express an opinion that was contrary to tradition. Even though the obedient attitude was encouraged from childhood and became a part of the fibre of the personality, on one occasion Kika found the courage to speak her thoughts.

"I don't want to get married so young," she protested. "I want to go to a school where I can learn hairdressing and then I want to work for a while. It's too early for me to marry."

Our parents were amused by Kika's outburst which was perhaps worse than if they had become angry. It just meant that they were not taking Kika's feelings seriously. Mother tried to reason with Kika by explaining what had been explained to herself when she was no more than a child by her own mother.

"It is right for a woman to marry early," she spoke persuasively.

"You will have a husband, your own home, children, nothing is more important. What good is school? You can be lead astray in such places. A woman can acquire a bad reputation if she is unmarried for too long."

While Mother was speaking these words, she appeared uncomfortable and even unconvinced by her own argument. Father then put an end to the discussion.

"Kika, we deeply love and care for you. You are very precious to us. No one has a better daughter and we are proud of you but on this issue, your mother is right. This is how your grandmothers married. This is how your mother and I married, and this is how you will marry. This is how the world is."

Kika listened to Father's words and then looked down at the floor without answering. I knew that she disagreed with Father but she would not argue with him. In later life, she spoke about how unfair it was that she should have married so young and against her true feelings, but she also expressed the understanding that Mother and Father did what they thought was best for her.

There was a formal process for the arranged marriage: the 'proxenetis' or the proposer acted on behalf of the young man and his family. He consulted with the family of the young woman regarding the possibility of introducing the young people for the purpose of marriage. This was followed by an initial meeting in which the parents of the couple discussed the matter. It was important at this meeting to go through, as sincerely as possible, everything that needed to be spoken about. It was a bad idea to try to withhold information that if it came to light could have an adverse effect on the future marriage. If all went well, the young man and woman had a first meeting accompanied by their families and they had a chance to see each other.

This is how events occurred in my sister's road to marriage. We were first visited by the Proxenetis with the father of the young man. They were welcomed to our home and they sat with my father in the living room where they talked. My mother made coffee and served it to the men then sat quietly and listened to the men discussing the matter. At the beginning, the conversation was informal but then the important questions were asked. These related to the age of the couple, their jobs, their characters and what help each would receive from their family.

"My son is a strong young man who does not shy away from work. He will work hard to support a wife and children."

By this he meant that his son would have to stand on his own feet and not expect financial help from him. Then it was my father's turn to speak about what he was able to offer.

"My daughter," he began, "is an able and hard-working girl who can earn good wages working as a seamstress. I can also help by allowing them to have a room in our flat and live here without contributing money so that they can save for the future."

This was my father's way of saying that my sister had no dowry. Eventually, the person who all this discussion was about, was called to the room with the pretext of asking her to make some more coffee. My sister entered looking shy and embarrassed. She was seventeen years old and, in many respects, no more than a child.

"This is our daughter Kika," my father introduced her with pride and one could see a Father's love in the expression on his face.

"Would you make us some more coffee, Kika?" my father added.

"Yes, Father," she answered obediently while all the time looking down and feeling too shy to meet anyone's eyes.

All went well at this first meeting. My father and our guest agreed that the two families should meet together so that the two young people should have a chance to see each other.

When the time came, the two families gathered together, the men were talking in one group while the women were conversing in another. Nobody spoke about the reason for the gathering, everyone acted as if they were devoid of such knowledge, but everyone knew the real reason and so the members of the young man's family were unobtrusively and kindly observing my sister. On the other hand, Mother was watching the young man like a hawk, trying to discover signs of any habits that might indicate that he would not be a suitable husband for my sister.

The custom was that after a day or so, the young people involved were asked if they really liked each other and if they were willing to marry. If both agreed, then matters went to the next stage. This was the formal *logiasma* or the giving of the word of promise. Though it appeared to be fair that both young people were consulted if they wanted to proceed in the matter, the nature of this arrangement coupled with the traditional village values of the parents must have meant that girls were exposed to coercion. I know that though my sister had already said that she didn't want to go through with it, matters were presented to her in such a manner, particularly by Father, that when it came to giving her answer, she was unable to refuse.

A short while after the *logisma* or the giving of the promise, the engagement was arranged. At this ceremony, a priest was invited to bless the engaged couple and to bless their engagement rings. The celebration was usually quite a big event to which friends and relatives were invited but it was the wedding, of course, that was the culmination of the events which were set in motion by the proxenetis enquiry.

The planning for the wedding took place almost immediately after the engagement. Dates were arranged, the church and reception hall would be booked. Invitations were printed out on very ornate cards and usually in gold print. For my sister's wedding, the invitation read:

'Mr and Mrs Loizou from Sotira, Famagusta, Cyprus and Mr and Mrs Ataou from Avgorou, Famagusta, Cyprus request the pleasure of your company at the wedding of their children Kika and George at All Saints Greek Orthodox Church.'

The number of guests was in the hundreds and each family was visited personally to be presented with the invitation from the couple or their parents. Such a custom wasn't a problem in a small village in Cyprus, but it was quite an undertaking if you lived in London. Yet, most families who planned the weddings of their children went through this laborious process of zigzagging across London to deliver the invitations.

My sister's wedding was typical of many. The couple went through the ancient ceremony standing before the altar. The church of All Saints in Pratt Street, Camden Town was crowded with men, women and children. Everyone was dressed in their best clothes. The men wore dark suits with stiffly starched white shirts and colourful ties. The women wore eye-catching dresses and high-heeled shoes with pointed toes. The witnesses, the *koumpari* and the *koumeres* stood in a circle around the alter with the bride and groom at the apex. The Orthodox Priests in their richly embroidered Byzantine cassocks busied themselves singing the marriage liturgy that seemed to go on forever. The icons of the Christ, the *Panayia* and the Apostles, forever frozen in their silent postures, looked down from the iconostasis as the couple were joined together in matrimony.

Following the religious ceremony, all travelled by car or coach to the reception hall which was the local town hall. The catering was prepared at home. Both families worked through the previous night at home to cook and then to deliver great quantities of meat balls, roasted chicken, salads and such usual dips as tahini, houmous and taramosalata. The tables were set with bottles of wine and whiskey and with an abundance of food. A live band with violin, bouzuki and drums entertained and went through a list of songs and dances which like every Cypriot wedding, culminated in the dance of the bride and bridegroom when the guests pinned money on them.

While the bride and bride groom celebrated their nuptial, their guests saw it as an opportunity to seek out friends and relatives at the party. It was a great get together where people ate, drank, danced but most of all, they talked and talked about their families and work, life in England or the Cyprus problem. Often it was a chance to catch up on the latest gossip. This is how so many Greek Cypriot men and women were married in London during the late 1950s and 1960s. With the increasing sophistication and the growing wealth of the community, this traditional village type wedding went through quite a change.

The young women who went through this process are now the mothers of grown-up children who are themselves parents. Most of these grandmothers share the common experience of the arranged marriage, and will also, probably, if they are not too embarrassed, confirm that on the morning after their wedding, the elders of the two families would inspect the bridal bed sheets to examine the proof that the bride had indeed been pure and a virgin on her wedding night. I remember very clearly on that morning how my sister's in-laws had arrived at our house very early.

Together with my parents, they entered the bedroom of the newly married couple. They were very composed because this was for them a very serious matter. When they remerged, they were full of smiles and happy tears. They hugged and kissed my sister who smiled back at them but seemed very uncomfortable and embarrassed by the whole process. From the point of view of these village people, family honour had been maintained and enhanced because the daughter had been given in marriage as a pure virgin and they had the evidence to prove it.

Thankfully for most of us, life has changed for the better and certainly the young women from our community now marry when they like and whom they like. I am happy that the Cypriots have learnt that there should be limits to certain traditions but sadly there are other communities in the United Kingdom who have not yet understood that their young people who have been born or have been raised here question and often are against the idea of the arranged marriage. How strange it must have seemed to the girls who had grown up in the United Kingdom and who had tasted the new permissive British culture to be expected to go through an arranged village marriage and worse still to be subjected to the post wedding night examination! Further, this is not yesterday's injustice inflicted on the young women of ethnic minority groups of long ago. We are not only speaking of young women who have recently arrived to the United Kingdom from far away villages in Pakistan or India. British teenagers from Islamic backgrounds are often taken for 'holidays' to India or Pakistan and when they arrive there, they are faced with an arranged marriage, often to a complete stranger. Some teenagers feel that they have to choose between the traditions of their families and their own new values that belong to the culture of the country that they now live in and think of as their own. It is a difficult choice, but some ethnic minority young women find the courage to make it. In some horrific cases, the families concerned will take matters to the extreme and inflict upon the rebellious young woman, as they see it, the ultimate punishment of death, justifying their obscene actions by claiming that the behaviour of their victim had brought dishonour upon the family.

1. The birth control pill – A history of the pill. *The Guardian.* Sarah Bridge. 12th September, 2007.
2. Roy Jenkins was appointed as Home Secretary in 1965. He led the movement for social reform in which he sought to change or

abolish laws that were not in keeping with a humanistic and civilised way of life. This included the abolition of capital punishment, theatre censorship, decriminalisation of homosexuality, changes that made abortion easier and safer and the banning of birching. However, the critics of Roy Jenkins have said that his reforms far from creating a 'civilised society', have in fact created a 'permissive society' in which family values and good manners have been replaced by promiscuity and loutish behaviour. Roy Jenkins, Europe and the Civilised Society. Professor Vernon Bogdanov, Gresham College, 25th January, 2013.

The Mother Tongue

Boys from the Greek Cypriot community did not face the same problems as their sisters. As boys, who had come to England as young children, we were very receptive to the new culture and were quickly anglicised. The most apparent sign of this in relation to my own individual experience was that my use of English after the age of about twelve or thirteen had already become fluent, rich and expressive while my use of the Greek Language had remained static and clumsy. For me and fellow Cypriot friends who had arrived together as very young children, English had now become our everyday language and we spoke it in school, on the streets and where ever we gathered together to play. Our parents were uncertain how they should face this sudden new phenomenon. For some strange reason, they had not bargained that their young children would be fluent speakers of English and only second rate speakers of Greek at best. They had probably naively thought that we would grow up as typical Cypriots right in the middle of London, oblivious to the life around us! Well, they were soon to be disappointed and it is a lesson that still needs to be learnt by those who have only recently arrived and who fanatically wish to enforce the customs and rules of faraway places on the children who are being raised in England. So, when our parents would look upon us at social gatherings, speaking English in a strong and confident manner while at the same time responding to them in the type of Greek that only a foreign person would utter, they often exclaimed,

"Speak in your own language as well, otherwise you will forget it."

They said this in a semi worried, semi-amused tone and of course, they already understood that the first serious loss of identity when you live as an ethnic minority far from your country of origin, is your language. This may happen in stages and it may take a generation or two but as surely as night follows day, it is one of the conclusions of moving from one country to another. There are a thousand and one reasons why we, the Cypriots, who came here as children or who were born here do not retain the old mother language. It might be worth mentioning some of those reasons.

The English language is phenomenally dynamic and at the same time easy to acquire. What made it very attractive for youngsters coming to live in England and to other people in general, is the fact that it is the language of the internationally influential American film industry. Almost all the world-famous film stars from the beginning of film making have been English speaking. In films, cowboys and Red Indians spoke in English, Roman emperors and pharaohs, gladiators, pirates, buccaneers, spacemen, magicians, slave girls, detectives and hoods, ladies, heroes of romance, comedians and dancers alike, all spoke in English. To understand the films, you have to understand the language. Our learning of English coincided with the release of such cinema classics as *Psycho*, *Lawrence of Arabia*, *The Good, the Bad and the Ugly*, *The Graduate*, *Spartacus*, *Dr No* and many more. We went to the cinema regularly, enjoyed the visual spectacle, the exciting sound effects, but most of all, we took in the language, following the dialogue so that we could understand the meaning of the plot and action of the film. It was a great way to learn a language and at the same time, enjoy some great films! There were other incentives: the songs of popular music were sung mainly in English. We hummed words, we tapped our feet to the rhythm of the music, we memorise the chorus and we learnt to sing the words of the great artists. We also learnt the language of the place for ordinary, everyday reasons like going to school, making friends and having a social life. It wasn't long before we were even thinking in English. What other outcome could there possibly be?

Part 4: Another Identity

The Change

It was more than fifty years ago that we embarked on a ship from a small picturesque port in Cyprus. We were a simple group of people, a family beginning a journey to England like many other families before us and as many others would follow in our wake. We were like a small wave, a part of a more general movement of people not only from Cyprus, but from other parts of the world in search of a better future, in search of a destiny that might provide hope and fulfilment of dreams. It is quite wonderful and restores some of our lost faith in the face of what is often a cruel world that some rich and powerful countries recognised the need to embrace the poor and the oppressed from troubled or devastated areas of the world. I know that some will say that it was not out of kindness and that these countries wanted cheap labour to feed their economies. That is true, but it must also be said that the immigrants were granted democratic rights. We became citizens, we had the right to vote, we could participate in education, in business, in the professions. We were offered hope when often in our own war-torn lands, we had none. The door was opened for us to enter and when we had stepped inside, we usually found hospitality and respect. There was some aversion to our arrival, but in the general scheme of things, the aversion was negligible. We were the tired and the poor in search of a new home, in search of work and hope. Yes, we were, but despite the reality of the circumstances, the notion that wealth would be gained and there would be a triumphant return to the motherland with pockets full of money. The emotional attachment to the old motherland was difficult to forget. The adults, mothers and fathers never doubted on the day of their departure from their native soil that one day, in the not so distant future, they would be leading their families like a Moses or an Aaron out of the bondage of north west European industrialised society with its ruthless Anglo Saxon work ethic, back to their easier going, Mediterranean promised land. The illusion was that they would return as the same people who had left, they and their children together, to reclaim their former lives with the difference that they would now have far more wealth, gained in the distant lands where they had sacrificed a few years so that they could live more easily in their own country. They would build houses, make suitable marriages for their children and have a better standard of life than their wealthy neighbours who had previously looked down upon them and who did not have to immigrate to improve their lives. They would live happily ever after, they thought and they dreamed. Alas, it was not to be.

Very few immigrants ever made the return journey. It might be an awkward decision to leave your country even when life is difficult but when you have done so and through hard work you have built a new home, made new relations, acquired a new language, where the death of old parents is mourned or marriage and the birth of a new generation is celebrated, then the thought of return begins to lack immediate importance and it is pushed further back in the order of priorities. Eventually, after many years, the thought of the return is something vague and is treated with a lack of conviction that it would ever happen. Where else would you belong except in the place where destiny has brought you, the place where you have worked and made a life for yourself? Millions of people, like the waves of the sea, relentlessly moved from east to west or from north to south, heading towards centres of economic wealth and activity. People went to America, Australia, Western Europe in search of work and a better life. Was there ever a mass return to the old nests, back across the wide sea? No, there was not. Such an undertaking seemed too difficult, too uncomfortable. Eventually, it is understood that it was a one-way journey; it was a one-way ticket of no return. Yet, even people like myself who have grown from childhood into adulthood in England, in some strange nostalgic moment, as if we cannot ever entirely dismiss the thought, may feel that we are far from home and may yearn to return to an experience that is no longer there. Such thoughts are quickly dismissed because we understand that we are clutching at fantasies as we realise at last that there has been a very gradual metamorphosis. It now feels as if it happened in secret, perhaps while we slept, in the dark, unobserved. Actually this is not the case; it happened while we were wide awake and in fact, we all in our own distinctive way wanted to blend, to adopt and to facilitate the metamorphosis. One might ask, why not, it's a very natural reaction: change according to the challenges of your environment or face extinction. I think that most people carry the instinct for survival in their genetic makeup and anyway, the metamorphosis was very much a creative, positive process in which many individuals found the possibility to achieve their potential and for the Cypriot community in the UK to gain a sense of identity that is different from the Cypriots of Cyprus.

At the beginning, the alteration was no more than a thin, cosmetic veneer. The clothes that were brought in the suitcase, the suit made by the local village tailor, the dress made by the village seamstress or the shoes cobbled by the village shoemaker soon wore out and were eagerly replaced by English fabrics and London fashions. Clothes and hairstyles were the first obvious changes and they related to outward appearance and projection of the self. But there were deeper and more significant changes that had to be made quickly and were essential for the sake of immediate economic survival and eventual prosperity: the mothers and the fathers who had made the journey and had arrived here mostly penniless now entered the factories of England to make a beginning in the financial security of their families. The rhythm of the day was determined by the clocking in and the clocking out at the factory entrance. The many religious holidays that had been enjoyed with festivities in the villages and towns of Cyprus were remembered but had to be mainly ignored except for those religious dates like Christmas and Easter that were shared with the British. There were also new words that had become permanent fixtures in the language of the new arrivals: 'please', 'thank you', 'marketa', 'buso'. Appearance, manners and language had suddenly taken on a slightly different hue, shape, tone and texture.

Undoubtedly, the very fibre of our identity had begun to change but it was so gradual, silent and unobtrusive that it was hardly noticed by even those who were undergoing the process. The change gathered momentum and it is still moving on. For us, who have been raised in England or who were born here, the experience of the migration lives on vaguely like a dream. We see ourselves as children holding our parents by the hand, leaving our troubled, fractured land behind in search of a new home, far away, in a distant country. This is the experience that the immigrant never forgets; the day of the departure from his home land, the journey and finally reaching his destination from which he imagines that one day he will return to find the place and the people that he had once left behind, not realising that the human condition is always in a state of flux and that nowhere and no group of people or individuals ever remain the same.

We crossed the ocean and underwent the metamorphosis that still continues. On this new stage, we played our part according to the scene and action of a different kind of play that is called England. Those who were left behind, also changed according to the circumstances that befell them. They had to face 1974 with all its tragic consequences. Our experiences were quite different so that now we feel more strongly the distance of geography, events and the passing of time and an acceptance of our fate. And now, who are we? What are we? For our parents, there were changes but they were not so deep and they held onto their often unrealised and unreal dreams of the return. But for us, who were brought here as babies or were born here and our children and grandchildren, because the generations role on unceasingly, how have we fared?

205

We have become a part of the London scene; we have blended almost fully but not entirely. It is not a matter of choice, a decision that is made, but rather it is a part of an evolutionary process, a dialectic that brings new realities into being.

The synthesis for the Cypriot community is not yet complete. We are still caught up in the in between period. In my opinion, British people have always tried to be fair to the immigrants who have arrived at these shores and we, the immigrants, have found safety, security and the opportunity to pursue and fulfil our goals in life. Yet, we still do not feel that we are entirely a part of the main; there is the feeling that we remain as islands surrounded by a beneficent British ocean whose waves gently massage our coastline, gradually eroding it. Perhaps, the umbilical cord with the old mother country is still attached to our emotions so that even for those of us who grew up in England or even for those who were born here, we cannot forget the roots of our origins and why should we? This can be seen by how devastated British Cypriots felt when in 1974, the Turkish army invaded Cyprus and murdered many ordinary people and effectively partitioned the island. British Cypriots organised themselves to offer whatever help they could to their unfortunate brethren on the island. I suppose this suggests that though our identity must belong to our present experience, our past has also an unforgettable and important bearing on our understanding of who we are.

The Tourist

Returning to Cyprus for me is always a special event and a journey which is always more than just a package holiday. At such times, I find myself thinking back to that life-changing outward journey from Cyprus to England that I made as a little boy so many years before. I remember that day very distinctly: my hand was tightly gripped by my mother as if I could somehow disappear from the face of the earth if she held my hand more loosely. I was excited that we were going to board a huge ship, the type that I had watched from the beach at Varosi, steaming by in the distance with black smoke churning out of its funnels. Boarding the ship was indeed a day of immense excitement like the days when we went to the paniyiri at Sotira or Stylloi and would stay with Grandmother or one of our aunties.

After we had boarded the ship, there was no return to the world that we had left behind; it changed beyond recognition and even to this day, if we travel to Cyprus, the return to Varosi, our home town, itself remains elusive and beyond possibility. We can only look on from afar with sadness and nostalgia at the city that has become a ghost, which only has life in our memories and the hope in our hearts that one day the barbed wire and the illegal occupation will come to an end.

There is also the memory of the Grandmother whose tears and anguish could not be hidden or disguised on the day of our departure while Grandfather sadly and silently looked at the ground. We would never see them again. But ahead of us lay the adventure of the journey that we made on what seemed to me a gigantic ship or the train that was like a dragon that cut across the land at high speed. More than the adventure of the journey was the adventure to establish ourselves in our new adopted land; to learn the language; to find jobs; go to school; make new friends; make new lives; be a part of what was for us a new society.

When we visit Cyprus for our holiday, I instinctively look for familiar places or familiar faces that might somehow connect to the life before our exodus. There are thankfully, up to this point in my story, some surviving aunts and uncles who have been blessed with good health and long life and whom I am always overjoyed to see again.

The saddest feature from the past is for me the sight of the ghost city of Varosi; from the village of Dherinia, it is no more than a stone's throw away. It is there like a wounded body waiting to be resuscitated. It appears from a distance, from across the barbed wire, from across the Dead Zone as the ceasefire line is called, lifeless and empty while the people of Cyprus wait in anticipation for the day of its resurrection. But Cyprus, despite all its endless political problems, despite the ghost city, has become modern, courageous and daring, full of talented, skilful and enterprising young people, hungry for success.

During our brief holidays on the island, we might be searching for a past and the people there often kindly tolerate our eccentricities because they know us and the background to our quests. A certain feeling or emotion that I experience whenever I return to Cyprus is that when I come out from arrivals at Larnaca Airport, I quite irrationally expect some kind of a welcome home reception, but there is no one there except the faces of strangers and taxi drivers waiting to take you to your holiday hotel. The friends, the uncles and aunts with their hordes of children who made such a noise, the sweet Grandmother who wept to see us go on the day of our exodus and the Grandfather with the sad down cast expression but with the big heart full of love are not there to renew the bonds that once held us together. There is a price that is paid for seeking a better life beyond one's native shores. At some point, the bonds between the old life and the new are surely and inevitably cut. The umbilical cord cannot hold forever.

We now return as tourists to what was once the place where we lived and where, if not for the decision to leave, our lives would have been totally different. When I arrive with my family, we are picked up by a taxi or sometimes there is a coach and we are taken to our hotel. This is all rather well organised, impersonal and I can't say that after a long flight we are not pleased with the efficiency of the locals. On most occasions, when we arrive at the hotel, we are further satisfied with the clean, comfortable rooms with the sea view. During these episodes in Cyprus, I try not to show that I am just a tourist but that I am also a local boy because it is usually apparent that we are from London, particularly through our clumsy use of the Greek language. In hearing our spoken Greek usage or observing our futile attempts to appear as natives, the locals might be provoked into a gentle laughter that stems from the genuine humour of the circumstances and in most cases, it is meant with sympathy and kindness.

My visits to Cyprus always invoke in my thoughts not only about my early childhood and about the people who were left behind but also about my life in the UK. This probably happens because on holiday one has the time of day to think and reflect about our past. Inevitably, I find that very often, my mind wanders back to events which I suppose were the most

208

important for me in my personal development. Thoughts of my school days, during which I was inspired by my wonderful teachers to learn and to love the English language and its great wealth of literature, come flooding back to me. This success at school enabled me to attend university and then to become a teacher. I remember my father saying that it was his greatest pride that he had a son who had graduated from an English university, from the University of London, Institute of Education and had become a teacher. He would sometimes say to me:

"Fotaki, it is a great and noble achievement to be a teacher because you are entrusted with the future of the younger generation. In my village…" he would continue speaking in a fond and gentle manner whenever reminiscing about pleasant memories from the past, "in my village, the teacher was greatly respected. The village people with children at school always took him presents for Christmas and Easter. They gave him a freshly slaughtered chicken, some halloumia and dried, rolled trahana for making soup. In the summer, the teacher's presents were fresh fruit and vegetables. Whenever he entered the kafenion, he was offered a chair immediately and a dozen men insisted on paying for his coffee. Yes, the teacher is always greatly respected."

When he thought about the past, it was his habit to stare silently in the space in front of him for a moment or two, as if evoking the picture of the memory in his mind. When satisfied, he would focus his eyes on the present, smile and continue his conversation. I suppose he had some romantic notion regarding the lives of teachers. He was speaking of another place, another time about an attitude that no longer existed. Little did he realise just how difficult the lives of teachers in London could be! Even in Cyprus, society has changed so much that my father's experience of school and the respect for teachers is something very different today from what he remembered and described. But I hear his melodic voice relating the stories of his life and times, stories from Sotira and Varosi and London. I see him laughing at every adversity that he confronted in his ever-optimistic attitude towards life.

Mothers, fathers, sisters, brothers, grandmothers, grandfathers, wives, husbands, friends, the list of people we have known stretches from our birth to our present across time and place. We evoke the images of the people who we have known, the people whom we love and sometimes the people who have caused us pain or discomfort. We hear their voices from the past, speaking clearly and audibly as if they are never far away, as if they are speaking to us here and now. They exist in our minds, those who have gone from us. We visualise their smile, we hear their voices, they are always a part of us. Certainly, you cannot separate the memory from the man and as I sit under the canopy of a beach café, looking out at the turquoise blue Mediterranean Sea, the realisation manifests itself more clearly than perhaps the previous year that this patch work of experiences I have expressed, that seem to have been woven together in slow motion, equal an important part of my life time and have given my personality form and structure. My experiences have defined my identity as both not quite a Cypriot, nor entirely British, but a synthesis of the two. I am truly what Cypriots now call the people who immigrated to England, I am an *Englezokypraios* or to translate, Englishcypriot. Sometimes, this feels like an awkward position to be in but most of the time I and others like me are happy and comfortable with our identity and who we have become as a result of having spent our lives in England. The question of identity is no longer an issue, neither for us nor for the people of the United Kingdom, with whom we have made our lives. We simply just get on with our everyday affairs without any longer thinking that the stage is in England and that we are somehow in the wrong kind of drama. In fact, our new roles in our new land feel very natural. It has taken many years to arrive at this new sense of identity and we now understand that identity is not only the memory of a history, it is also the feeling of a natural interaction with your present environment and the sense that you belong to it more than to any other place.

This sense of belonging can manifest itself in many ways but for me it is through an attachment to a particular scene or place, a geographical location. One such experience is when after some visit abroad, our aeroplane begins to descend over the Home Counties revealing the rolling hills of southern England, sometimes basking in sunshine, with lush green fields divided with hedge groves in unparalleled neatness. My memory then goes back to the little boy who once journeyed with his mother and sister on a train that sped through a land of luxuriant green fields, in which herds of fat cattle and flocks of woolly sheep pastured beneath a blue sky, dappled with fluffy cotton clouds. This scene always prompts me to think that while other places have beauty, the beauty of England is indeed unique, and this uniqueness also extends into the great metropolis where one of my favourite places in London is Parliament Hill, near Highgate. When on occasion I happen to visit this location, as I stand at the summit of the hill on a clear day, looking across the panorama of this vast, majestic city, picking out the familiar land marks of Saint Paul's Cathedral, Big Ben, The Post Office Tower and further east, the buildings of Canary Wharf confidently thrusting their towers into the skyline, I sense the dynamic vitality of this great, beating heart that I first felt as a little boy who journeyed from a distant land, on a one way ticket to London, London the city I now call my home.

~